Sew
Fabulous Fabric

Sew
Fabulous Fabric

ALICE BUTCHER & GINNY FARQUHAR

D&C
David and Charles
www.mycraftivity.com

A DAVID & CHARLES BOOK
Copyright © David & Charles Limited 2008

David & Charles is an F+W Publications Inc. company
4700 East Galbraith Road
Cincinnati, OH 45236

First published in the UK in 2008
First published in the US in 2008

Text and designs copyright © Alice Butcher and Ginny Farquhar 2008
Photography and illustrations copyright © David and Charles 2008

A catalogue record for this book is available from the British Library.

ISBN-13: 978-0-7153-2858-3 paperback
ISBN-10: 0-7153-2858-1 paperback

Printed in China by SNP Leefung
for David & Charles
Brunel House   Newton Abbot   Devon

Head of Publishing: Ali Myer
Desk Editor: Bethany Dymond
Designer: Mia Farrant
Project Editor: Nicola Hodgson
Production Controller: Bev Richardson
Illustrator: Helen Philipps
Photographers: Simon Whitmore and Karl Adamson

Visit our website at www.davidandcharles.co.uk

David & Charles books are available from all good bookshops; alternatively you can contact our Orderline on 0870 9908222 or write to us at FREEPOST EX2 110, D&C Direct, Newton Abbot, TQ12 4ZZ (no stamp required UK only); US customers call 800-289-0963 and Canadian customers call 800-840-5220.

Introduction

Recycling has become a buzzword in the last few years, but previous generations have been saving fabrics, clothing, furnishings, buttons and trimmings for centuries. Nothing was ever wasted: worn-out shirts and dresses were cut up and made into patchwork quilts or wall hangings, and fabric scraps were used to make rag rugs. Many of you may remember the excitement of rummaging through your grandmother's button boxes for the prettiest buttons that had been snipped off old dresses, shirts and jackets to be used again.

Our own personal love affair with recycled fabrics started in earnest when we began working together in around 2001. Having both been passionate collectors of fabrics and notions for many years, this collaboration inspired us to push our ideas and creativity even further.

Sew Fabulous Fabric is a beautiful book, full of colour and inspiration and practical, achievable projects. Whether you are an experienced sewer or just love fabrics and are itching to start creating with them, then this book is for you. Some of the projects are perfect for an adult and child to work through and make together, so, whatever your skill level, you can share our approach, techniques and ideas of using collected and recycled fabrics to transform your surroundings.

Taking our own daily lives as inspiration, we offer you 20 exciting projects with the aim of giving you the confidence and know-how to enter into your own personal adventure with fabric. We have divided our projects into four themed sections.

Home Making features projects to bring homemade charm to your everyday surroundings. Add warmth and colour to your home with some gorgeous patchwork draught excluders (pages 36–39), or revitalize an interior with stylish curtains complete with appliquéd motifs (pages 40–45). Liven up the daily chores of cooking and laundry with the baking day aprons (pages 26–31) and the pretty peg bag (pages 32–35).

Out and About concentrates on transforming your favourite scraps of fabric and old clothing into glamorous and practical accessories. Show off your sewing skills and creativity wherever you go! The rucksacks (pages 52–57) are ideal for throwing in everything you need to set off for a country walk. Liven up every outfit you own by creating complementary corsages (pages 66–69), or make a beautiful matching handbag (pages 62–65).

Let's Celebrate is all about making original pieces to celebrate special times. The handmade cards (pages 84–87) and scented decorations (pages 88–91) make simple but beautiful gifts for any time of year. The treat bags (pages 80–83) can be made for specific holidays such as Halloween and Easter. The party table linen (pages 76–79) will turn any mealtime into an occasion, while the festive flags (pages 72–75) will add atmosphere wherever you hang them.

Lasting Memories is dedicated to more precious projects that might over time become family heirlooms. Preserve your child's artwork by using it as the inspiration for a special cushion (pages 98–101). Create a height chart out of recycled fabrics to keep a record of your children growing up (pages 106–109). Finally, celebrate Christmas every year by making personalized stockings for every member of the family (pages 94–97).

So start your own fabric journey and have lots of fun on the way!

Fabulous Fabrics

Apart from the ecological implications, recycling fabrics can be great fun! Recycled fabrics come in a variety of exciting, colourful and original patterns and textures and have a pleasing time-worn softness. Hunting through thrift shops or jumble sales is very satisfying, especially when you find a real gem. You can derive great pleasure from creating 'something from nothing'!

Whether it is vintage or six months old, an old woollen coat, a pair of curtains or an item of sentimental value, you will discover how to look for the possibilities and inspiration in any piece of fabric. We suggest ways of incorporating your finds into the projects, but remember that your creation, because it uses reclaimed fabrics, will be totally unique.

Sourcing fabrics

First, look around your home. Most of us have scraps of fabric around, maybe left over from shortening trousers, from previous dressmaking projects or from old drapes that have been replaced. You may have put aside some torn clothes to repair that are still sitting there, or have a favourite shirt that is in good condition except for an ink stain on the pocket. Some of you may have inherited precious pieces of fabrics or garments that you love but have kept in a box or drawer never to see the light of day. All of these items are the makings of the start to your fabric collection.

Start looking in thrift stores. Clothing and furnishings are brought in all the time, so there will always be something new for you to acquire for your stash. Other places to look are antique markets, flea markets and car boot sales – be prepared to barter in these places. Also keep an eye open for seasonal sales and the remnant table in your local fabric store; we have found some fabulous bargains in this way.

Colour and pattern

Mixing pattern and colour is a very personal choice. Try to experiment with your fabrics to arrive at a result that pleases you rather than following our suggestions rigidly. Find inspiration for each project in your own collection and let the fabrics lead you. We have included lots of suggestions for colour and fabric choice in the Fabric Focus section of each project to give you further ideas.

Patterns, plaids and plains can be mixed together, but try to have a common colour link between each of them. Don't disregard combining light- and heavy-weight fabrics together; just ensure that you mount the light-weight piece to give it more substance. Colour tones of the same shade work very well together. You can also achieve great effect from bright contrasting colours. Themes such as florals, polka dots or stripes are always successful.

Tip

To preserve the life of your fabrics, wash and iron them before storing them in a dry place. Fold and organize them by colour for easier reference.

Fabric types

Here are some of the basic fabric types and where you might salvage them from.

Cotton

The most popular cottons we use are lawns, ginghams, corduroys, denims, canvas and velvet. These can be sourced from shirts, dresses, jeans, skirts and bed linen.

Linen

Fine linen has a lovely quality that is particularly nice to use with heirloom projects. Sources are embroidered table linen, sheets, dresses and fabric lengths.

Wool

Wool is soft and snug with a lovely texture. If washed hotter than the recommended care label it can be felted and cut up for use in smaller projects. Good sources are suits, skirts, coats, knitted sweaters, blankets and scarves.

Silk

Silk always looks luxurious. Our favourites are doupion, crêpe de chine, noile and habutai. Doupion is a raw silk with a slub, often produced in India, and comes in a wide range of vibrant colours. It is commonly used in bridal and evening wear. Crêpe de chine is a beautiful weight of silk with a gorgeous drape. Noile is a roughly woven silk with a similar texture to linen. Habutai is a very fine silk available in a wide range of colours and commonly used for lining. You can source these fabrics from old ballgowns and bridesmaids' dresses, skirt linings and blouses.

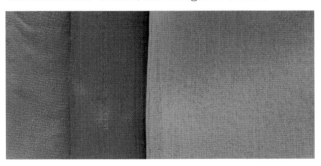

Determining your fabric

If you have bought a vintage fabric without a care label and are unsure of what the fabric is, the easiest way to determine this is with a simple burn test.

Cut a small square (approx 2.5cm/1in) from the fabric and hold it between a pair of tweezers. Ignite the fabric over a non-flammable surface in a well-ventilated room. The way it reacts will tell you the fabric content.

- **Wool** smells of burning hair or feathers and the flame will self-extinguish. Its ash is blackish and turns to powder when crushed.
- **Silk** burns slowly and smells of burning hair or feathers. It self-extinguishes. Its ash is greyish and turns to powder when crushed.
- **Cotton** smells of burning paper. It has a slow-burning ember and its ash is grey and cobwebby.
- **Linen** behaves in a similar way to cotton but takes longer to ignite.
- **Polyester** has a sweet smell. It gives off black smoke and rolls up into a hard, shiny black bead.
- **Acetate** smells acidic or vinegary. It will continue to burn after a flame source is removed and rolls into a hard black bead.
- **Acrylic** gives off an acrid smell. It will continue to burn after a flame source is removed and melts to a hard black crust.

Basic Tool Kit

You'll find that each project has a You Will Need list. This is a list of materials and equipment required in addition to the basic tool kit listed here. We hope that most of the equipment in the basic toolkit consist of items already in your sewing box but if not, try to add them. This really isn't a long shopping list, but we do recommend that you have these items before you begin! There is nothing worse than starting a project and then realizing that you don't have a vital piece of equipment.

Sewing machine
This is essential, as nearly every project in the book requires machine stitching.

Machine needles
- **Size 70** (9) for silks and fine cottons **(a)**.
- **Size 100** (16) leather needles **(b)**.
- **Size 90** (14) for denims, canvas and heavy-weight linens **(c)**.

Hand-sewing needles
- **Beading needles** for beading **(a)**.
- **Large-eyed chenille needles** to thread twine for beaded decorations **(b)**.
- **Straw needles** – they are long and strong so will stitch through canvas or denim but are fine enough to bead and embroider with **(c)**.

Equipment for drafting patterns
- **Pattern paper** is indispensable for drafting up patterns. Dot and cross paper is great if you can get it, but otherwise brown paper will do.
- **Paper and card** – you can recycle printed material or old cereal packets to make templates.
- **Tape measure**.
- **Ruler** – ideally a metal ruler giving both metric and imperial measurements.
- **Set square** – this is really useful for drafting patterns.
- **HB pencil**, **marker pen** and **sticky tape**.
- **Medium-weight calico** – this is a very useful multi-purpose cloth especially suitable for mocking up patterns and making toiles.

Pins
- General **dressmakers' pins** with glass heads.
- Extra-fine **bridal and lace pins** for delicate fabrics.
- **Safety pins** for turning through channels or pinning projects together.

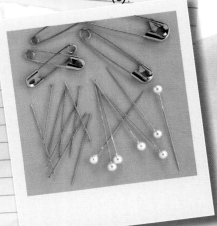

Scissors

- **Dressmaking shears** should be used only for cutting out fabric.
- **Pinking shears** cut a zigzag edge that can be used to neaten seams or give a decorative edge.
- **General-purpose scissors** for cutting out patterns, twine and for general use.
- **Embroidery scissors** for fine work and intricate cutting.

Sewing threads

- **General-purpose polyester sewing thread** is ideal for machine sewing and hand-sewing and comes in a kaleidoscope of colours.
- **Topstitching thread** is great for quilting.

Embroidery threads

Embroidery threads are widely available and come in a huge range of colours. We generally split them down into two threads, which means that one skein can last a long time!

Storage

- **Large envelopes** are useful for keeping all your pattern pieces together and can be filed easily.
- A **clear plastic box** with a lid or an empty drawer is useful for storing all of your projects and keeping them clean, safe and in one place.

Pressing equipment

- **Iron and ironing board**. You'll probably have these already, but if you are thinking of buying a new iron, keep the old one (unless it's unsafe) to use for crafting or fusing Bondaweb, as the glue can ruin a good iron.
- **Sleeve board** – this is useful for pressing seams and details, particularly on narrow sections.
- A **pressing cloth** is essential. It needn't be expensive – just a large square of muslin that will help protect your fabric and your iron.

Tailor's chalk

You can get chalk pencils as well as the traditional triangular chalk tablets; these are great for marking out stitching lines for embroidery as you have greater control and can achieve a finer line.

Bondaweb

Double-sided fusable webbing (Bondaweb) is essential for applying appliqué motifs and is great for all craft projects.

Staflex

Staflex is a cotton fusable interfacing/interlining. We use it for adding body to flimsy fabrics or for creating greater strength on straps (for example, on the Baking Days aprons – pages 26–31).

Fabric spray adhesive

Fabric spray adhesive such as Odif is a useful product, as it temporarily places a fabric, thereby enabling you to move it around if necessary. It also removes the chore of basting your quilting, although we wouldn't recommend using it as a substitute on a large quilt or hanging.

Stuffing

We recommend toy stuffing, but the polyester hollow fibre from a pillow or cushion is also suitable. Ensure that it carries a fire safety kite mark.

Stitch and Tear

Stitch and Tear is a useful product for creating embroidered text or detail on a project. With a pencil, draw your design onto the stitch and tear, pin in position, embroider on top of the pencil line and, once complete, tear away to leave the finished design.

Basic Techniques

This section gives you a guide to all the techniques that you will need to make the projects featured within this book.

Drafting a pattern and scaling up templates

The patterns and motifs in this book can be found on pages 116–125 and need to be scaled up on a photocopier. Your local library or printers can help with this. We have given the percentage that they need to be enlarged by. The motifs, however, can be used in any of the projects and will need to be scaled up and down accordingly. For Time for a Treat (pages 80–83) and the larger pieces on the height chart (pages 106–109) we have given accurate measurements for the fabric requirements in the You Will Need list and therefore pattern pieces are not included. These have been highlighted for your reference. Transfer your patterns onto dot and cross paper or brown paper. Include all balance marks, grainlines and pattern placements.

Preparing the fabric

We would advise you to pre-wash your fabrics prior to cutting out to allow for any shrinkage that might occur. If you are using a cotton lining or interfacing you should pre-wash this too. For delicate fabric such as silk and wool that cannot be washed, you can gently tighten the fibres by hovering a steam iron 3–4cm (1¼–1¾in) above the cloth. Once you have completed this process the fibres shouldn't shrink any further.

Pattern symbols

Seamline

Where you sew the pieces together. Our projects all allow for a 1cm (³⁄₈in) seam allowance.

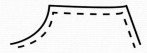

Straight grain

This indicates the lengthwise straight grain parallel to the selvedge and ensures that you cut out correctly.

Notches

These are used to mark and match corresponding seamlines.

Buttonholes

These indicate the placement of buttons and buttonholes.

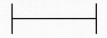

Pinning

General dressmakers' pins are suitable for most fabrics, although silks and fine cotton should be pinned with bridal or lace pins and heavy fabrics such as canvas and leather will need a more durable pin. When pinning your pattern onto your fabric, pin the straight grain first (if you do not pin on the straight grain you may encounter problems while sewing up as the fabric will have too much ease). Then pin around the pattern piece, diagonally at the corners and vertical to the pattern edge.

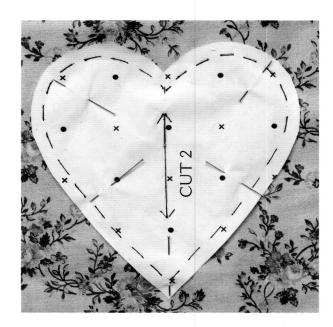

Markings

These are used to illustrate the position of decorative finishes and pockets. They can be translated onto the fabric with either tailor's chalk or a tailor tack.

Cutting

It is always important when cutting out to have a clean, large flat surface to work on. Ensure that your dressmaking scissors are sharp. To cut accurately, position your fabric to the left of your shears (or to the right if you are left-handed), take your time and follow the edge of the pattern line, taking confident long strokes for straight edges and shorter strokes for curved areas.

Standard machine-sewing stitches

Below we explain the four main types of stitch you will most often need to use on your sewing machine to complete the projects in this book.

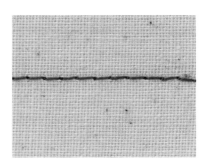

Straight stitch

All sewing machines will sew straight stitch, and it is the machine stitch that you will most commonly use. It is used in this book for sewing seams, topstitching and understitching. Unless otherwise stated, we would recommend that you set your stitch length to 2.5mm (¹⁄₈in). This gives a tidy, even stitch.

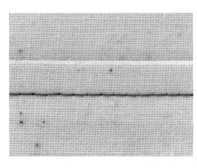

Topstitching

Topstitching is straight stitch set at about 3mm (³⁄₁₆in) length. It can be both decorative and functional while holding the seam firmly in place. We use it mainly on straps, pockets and waistbands. Place the machine foot to the edge of the seam and use this as a guide to keep the stitching following a straight line.

Zigzag

Zigzag is a versatile stitch and is used extensively in this book. It is used to neaten seams and edges. We also use it as a decorative edge and to hold appliqué motifs in position. To neaten seams, we suggest setting your zigzag to 2mm (¹⁄₁₀in) width and 2mm (¹⁄₁₀in) length. For using on appliqué, we suggest setting your zigzag to 2mm (¹⁄₁₀in) width and between 0.5mm and 1mm (¹⁄₄₀–¹⁄₂₀in) length.

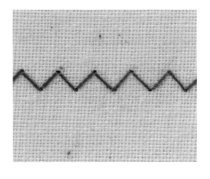

Understitching

Understitching is used to keep facings and linings from rolling and becoming visible from the front. Trim back seam allowances to about 3mm (³⁄₁₆in) and press to the side where the understitching is to be applied. Working from the right side, using a straight stitch, sew close to the pressed seam (approx 2mm/¹⁄₁₀in). The facing/lining can then be turned under, pressed and will lie flat.

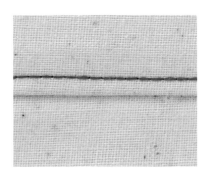

Standard hand-sewing stitches

Below we explain the six main types of hand-sewing stitches that you will need to know in order to complete the projects featured in this book.

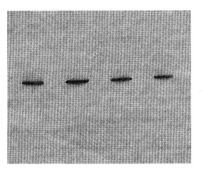

Running stitch

Running stitch is a short, even stitch that can be used for tacking, gathering and as a quilting stitch. Work from right to left, taking the needle in and out of the fabric and pulling the thread through. Keep your stitches small and evenly spaced.

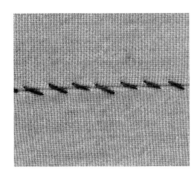

Oversewing

Oversewing is used to sew a fine seam. We use it mainly to sew up the gap when an item such as a decoration has been turned through. Make sure that the seam is turned in and, ensuring that the two folds are level and working from the right, make small even stitches over the seam at regular intervals. Oversewing can also be used as a decorative embroidery stitch.

Tacking

Tacking (basting) stitch is a longer, temporary running stitch used to hold fabric pieces together while making up. It can be removed once the permanent stitching is completed.

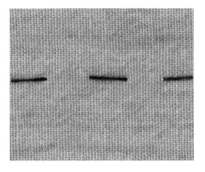

Slipstitch

Slipstitch is used to hem and also to close gaps in seams. Work from right to left, picking up a tiny piece of the fabric from one seam edge with the needle. Insert the needle into the other seam fold and move the needle along the fold 3mm (³/₁₆in). Push the needle out into the seam edge and repeat.

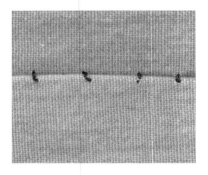

Tailor tacking

Tailor tacking is a temporary way of marking balance marks, pockets, darts or decorative placements. The stitches can be removed once the project is complete. Thread a needle and pull the thread ends level. Make a small stitch through the symbol, pattern paper and fabric and pull the thread through, leaving a 1.5cm (½in) end. Make another stitch over the first, leaving a large loop. Clip the ends and loop.

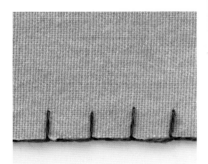

Blanket stitch

Blanket stitch is a decorative stitch that is commonly used to cover the edges of a fabric. Working from left to right, secure the thread and bring it out below the edge. Insert the needle through the fabric (about 4mm/³/₁₆in across and 4mm/³/₁₆in up) and bring out at the edge, keeping the thread from the previous stitch under the point of the needle. Pull the thread tight to form the stitch over the edge.

Seams

Below we explain the two types of seam neatening that we employ in the projects, together with advice on clipping and notching to create more professional seams.

Zigzag

We use machine zigzag stitch to neaten seams. Although there are different ways of using this method, in this book we set the zigzag to 2mm (¹/₁₀in) width and 2mm (¹/₁₀in) length. Trim the seam to 5mm (¼in) and zigzag both edges together.

Fell seam

Fell seams are commonly used in denim jeans or on a seam that is likely to get a lot of wear. This seam also gives a neat decorative finish. Stitch the seams w/s together. Trim one edge to 3mm (³/₁₆in). Press both edges to one side with the larger one covering the smaller. Turn in the larger edge by 5mm (¼in), press, pin and topstitch close to the folded edge.

Clipping and notching

Clipping (slits cut into the seam allowance) and notching (triangular wedges cut out of the seam allowance) are essential to many of the projects. It reduces bulk and helps a seam to curve or a corner to reach a tight point. The general rule is that if you wish the outer edge of the seam to give or spread, you should clip.

If you want to reduce the bulk of the outer edge of the seam, you should notch. With both techniques, hold the scissor points just short of the seam line to avoid cutting the stitches. An inward corner should be notched. Trim an outward corner across the point.

Sewing terminology and abbreviations

R/S: Right side (s)
W/S: Wrong side (s)
S/A: Seam allowance

Pressing

Pressing is an essential process for any sewing project and should be done at each stage of the making up. It should not be confused with ironing, which is when the iron glides over the fabric surface. Pressing is when the iron is pressed lightly down onto the fabric, lifted and moved onto the next area. Pins and tacking stitches should be removed before pressing and you should always use a pressing cloth (preferably muslin) so that you do not mark the fabric. Steam gives assistance when pressing thick or crease-prone fabrics, but wait until the fabric has cooled and dried before moving onto the next stage. Use the heat settings on your iron according to the fabric type.

Double-sided fusable webbing

Double-sided fusable webbing (Bondaweb) is an iron-on fabric adhesive that comes on peel-off paper backing. It is an essential part of our equipment when used for appliqué. Draw the motif onto the paper backing in pencil, remembering that if the design has an obvious direction it has to be drawn in reverse. Cut roughly around the shape, leaving a margin of about 5mm (¼in) outside the pencil line. With a medium-hot iron (no steam) fuse the Bondaweb, paper side up, onto the w/s of your fabric. Cut out the motif and peel off the backing paper. Place the motif, glue side down, onto the fabric on which it is going to be fused. Fuse using a pressing cloth.

Machine appliqué

Appliqué is the technique of applying fabric shapes to a background fabric to create surface decoration. There are a number of different types of appliqué, but the method that we use in this book is machine appliqué using a fusable webbing (Bondaweb) to apply the design (as described above). With a machine zigzag stitch set at 2mm width (¹⁄₁₀in) and 0.5mm–1mm length (¹⁄₄₀in–¹⁄₂₀in), zigzag very carefully around the outside edge of the motif to secure.

Buttons and buttonholes

Many modern sewing machines have a foot attachment that works out the size of the buttonhole for you. However, older models usually have built-in buttonhole stitch and a special foot that comes with the machine. We would advise you to check your sewing machine manual for instructions on how to create buttonholes. It is important to mark out the positioning (and if necessary the length marks) before commencing sewing. When you have completed your buttonhole, take a sharp pair of embroidery scissors and cut down the centre line between the stitching, taking care not to snip through the stitches.

Note that there are two different types of buttons, shank and sew-through, as explained below.

Shank buttons

Shank buttons stand slightly proud and are good for heavier-weight fabrics. To sew on a shank button, first make a few stitches on the top side of the fabric. Hold the button a little away from the fabric and bring the thread through the hole in the shank and the fabric three times. On the last stitch, bring the thread up through the button and then wind around the stitches to form a shank. Finish on underside.

Sew-through buttons

Sew-through buttons have two or four holes that are sewn through to apply the button to the fabric. Make a stitch where the button is to be positioned. Again, hold the button a little away from the fabric and sew through the holes into the fabric three times (if the button is four-holed, work the stitches over in a bar rather than a cross). Lift the button away from the fabric and wind the thread around the stitches. Finish on underside.

Turning through channels

By far the easiest way to turn through a channel or strap is to take a safety pin and fasten it into one of the open ends of the channel. Start to push the safety pin down through the centre of the channel so it starts turning in on itself. Keep feeding the safety pin along through the inside until it surfaces at the other end. Turn the remaining fabric through. Roll the seam edge between your fingers and thumbs to roughly create the shape of the strap and press.

Embellishments

Embroidery, buttons, trimmings and beading are all wonderful ways to add a final beautiful touch to your sewing project. You might be lucky enough to have inherited a well-established button box and trimming collection, but if you are starting from scratch, keep your eye out at charity shops, flea markets and antique fairs. Once you start searching, you'll be amazed at the treasures you can find! Below we also introduce some pretty embroidery stitches for you to experiment with.

Embroidery

Embroidery is a lovely way to add a unique finishing touch to a hand-sewn project. Embroidery silks come in a broad range of colours. Each stitch can be used to give a different effect and with a little practice is fairly easy to achieve.

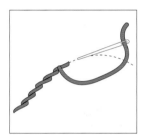

Stem stitch
Stem stitch is very useful for creating an outline. Work from left to right along the design, taking small stitches. The needle and thread should always come out on the left side of the previous stitch.

Backstitch
Backstitch can be used for creating outlines or embroidering letters and numbers. Insert the needle onto the design. Take a backward stitch and then bring the needle up a little way ahead of the first stitch. Insert the needle into the point where the first stitch began.

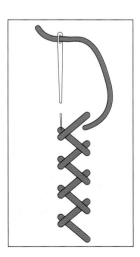

Herringbone stitch
Here we use herringbone as a purely decorative stitch, but it can also be used for hemming. Bring the needle up on the lower line at the left side. Insert on the upper line to the right and with the thread below the needle, take a small stitch to the left. Then insert the needle onto the lower line to the right with the thread above the needle and take another small stitch to the left. Continue to the end.

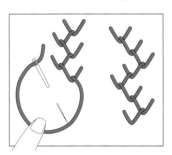

Feather stitch
Feather stitch is a beautiful decorative stitch that can be used as an edging. Bring the needle out at the top centre. Holding the thread down with your thumb, insert the needle to the right on the same level and take a small stitch to the centre, keeping the thread under the needle point. Inserting the needle a little to the left on the same level, take a small stitch to the centre. Repeat these two stitches, alternating between left and right.

Chain stitch
Chain stitch is a versatile decorative stitch. Bring the thread out and hold down with the left thumb. Insert the needle where it last emerged and bring the point out a little way in front. Pull through, keeping the thread under the needle point to form the looped stitch.

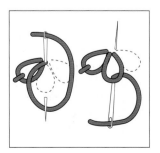

Lazy daisy
Lazy daisy is a delightful technique used to create simple flower designs. Work in the same way as chain stitch but fasten each loop at the foot with a small stitch. Work in a group to create flower petals.

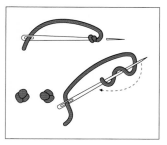

French knots

French knots can be used to give details to eyes, stamens or used in clusters to break up a surface. Bring the thread to the front and hold it down with the left finger and thumb. Twist the thread around the needle twice. Insert the needle close to where the thread emerged and draw the thread tightly through, creating a neat knot on the surface.

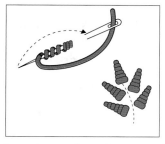

Bullion stitch

Bullion stitch is similar to a French knot, but you may vary the length of the knot. Insert the needle the appropriate distance from the original point, bring it back up through the first point, keep the needle in the material and twist the thread evenly around the needle the required number of times. Tighten the coil by pulling the thread and insert the needle into the end of the knot.

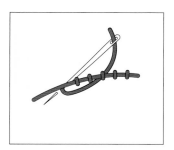

Couching stitch

Couching stitch is an effective way of creating a bold line. Lay a thread along the line of the design and, with another thread, tie it down at even intervals with a small stitch.

Buttons

All buttons can be useful; even plain brown shirt buttons could be used, for example, to add the eye detail to a decorative bird. When collecting clothing for use in your projects, get into the habit of removing all the buttons first so these can be reused too. When you're out and about, look for unusual colours, shapes and styles. Vintage and retro buttons look great on handbags and brooches.

Beads

Beads are perfect for all kinds of embellishment. Seed beads, scattered randomly, can be used to highlight a fabric, while larger glass beads work well strung together to add decorative detail on fabric hearts and stars. Broken or old necklaces often yield interesting and unusual beads.

We use the simplest of beading techniques by applying each bead individually. Using either a beading needle or very fine straw needle, thread a length of multi-purpose sewing thread in a colour that matches your chosen beads. Starting from the back, bring the needle through to the right side of the fabric, pick up a bead and slip it on to the needle and thread. Make a backstitch through the fabric (as close to the bead as possible) to hold in position and bring the needle out where you want to position the next bead. Continue until completed.

Trimmings

Trimmings such as ribbons, ric rac, woven braids and lace are readily available, but you can also salvage these from clothing and linens. Children's clothing is often trimmed with pretty ribbons and braids that can be cut off and reused. Ric rac gives a nostalgic feeling and adds fun and colour to any project. Vintage table linen, handkerchiefs and antimacassars often have beautiful lace edgings that can be removed, wound around card and stored in a trimmings box.

Home Making

This section focuses on bringing a touch of homemade beauty and charm to our everyday surroundings, and using handmade items to liven up daily chores and activities. Use these projects to get inspired and transform your house into a home, full of objects made by you that have real meaning for you.

We were inspired by the bounty of harvest time and our pleasure in home baking to make aprons – in both child size and adult versions – complete with motifs of wheat sheaves and loaves (pages 26–31). Try cheering up the drudgery of doing the laundry with a pretty little peg bag, complete with appliquéd garments on an embroidered washing line (pages 32–25). Made in crisp blues and yellows, you can almost smell the aroma of springtime-fresh laundry!

Keep your home warm and cosy with a beautiful patchwork draft excluder, and have fun decorating it with your favourite beads, buttons and embroidery stitches (pages 36–39). Be inspired by the possibilities of reusing fabric scraps by making colourful patch motifs to liven up clothing and bags (pages 22–25). Refurbish your interiors with homemade curtains, featuring appliquéd motifs stitched on to shop-bought base fabrics (pages 40–45). You can even create your own hand-crafted artworks to add a really personal and individual touch to your walls (pages 46–49).

Make Do and Mend

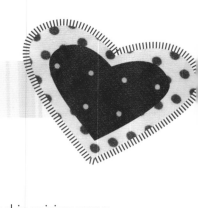

Patches are a great way to get into recycling and reusing fabrics in fresh and inspiring ways. You can make patches to use up your old scraps or remnants of fabric rather than just throwing them away; you can also use them to liven up or repair worn clothing, accessories or furnishings. Patches also make fabulous little presents – they're easy to slip into a card! This is a great starter project that would also be ideal for an adult and child to tackle together: kids will love customizing their clothes or school bags with these patches. We have chosen an ever-popular heart motif for our patch, but we have suggested other motifs to kick-start your imagination (see pages 24–25).

The appliqué techniques used here form the basis of many of the projects throughout the book. Appliqué is the technique of applying fabric shapes to a background fabric to create surface decoration. There are a number of appliqué methods; our preferred method is machine appliqué using a fusable webbing to apply the design, which is then finished with a machine zigzag stitch.

Fabric focus

If the patch is going to be practical, for example to cover up a worn-out area on the knees of jeans, you will need to use durable fabric such as denim, canvas or corduroy. We used two medium-weight cottons, with scarlet and white polka-dot patterns for visual impact. If the patch is going to be purely decorative, you could use more delicate fabric, such as printed cotton lawn, silk doupion or velvet.

You will need

- Two scraps of fabric in contrasting colours/patterns
- Piece of medium-weight felt 14 x 14cm (5½ x 5½in)
- Double-sided fusable webbing (Bondaweb)
- Polyester sewing thread
- Embroidery threads
- Pressing cloth

Tip

Bondaweb (Wonder Under) is an iron-on fabric adhesive that comes on peel-off paper backing. Appliqué shapes can be drawn accurately onto the paper and, when fused and cut out, the fabric shape remains crisp.

One Draw two heart-shaped templates (one smaller, one larger) onto a piece of pattern paper. Cut the templates out and trace around them in pencil onto the smooth side of the fusable webbing. Cut roughly round the shape, leaving a margin of about 5mm (¼in) outside the pencil line.

Two Take the two pieces of fabric you're using for the patch. Place the larger Bondaweb shape pencil-side up onto the wrong side of your first fabric in a position that gives you the best pattern coverage. Cover with a pressing cloth to protect your iron from any glue residue and, using the medium setting, press (fuse) for about 15 seconds until the shape is secure. Repeat with the second, smaller shape. Cut out both heart shapes along the pencil lines.

Three Peel the paper backing off the smaller heart, position it carefully in the centre of the large heart shape with a pin and fuse. **(a)**.

Four Peel the paper backing off the large heart, place it onto the piece of felt and fuse. Next, set your sewing machine to the standard straight stitch (see page 13) and, starting at the top middle point, stitch around the large heart, 2mm (¹/₁₀in) from the outer edge. Then, using sharp scissors, trim back the felt to the fabric edge **(b)**.

Five Now set your sewing machine to zigzag for appliqué stitching (see page 16) and zigzag around the edge of your shape. Choosing an embroidery thread that picks up a colour within your design (we used white to stand out against the scarlet), blanket stitch around the smaller heart (see page 14).

a

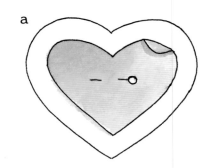

b

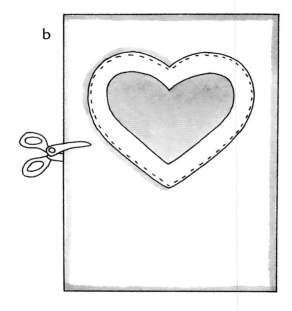

These patches make wonderfully vibrant and colourful additions to children's clothing. If you don't want to use a sewing machine to make the patch, simply follow steps 1–3, neaten the edges with blanket stitch or pinking shears and sew the patch in place using running stitch. We've suggested using motifs of a snail, a star, a butterfly and a flower.

Six We finished this project off by carefully pinning the patch to a pocket and then sewing it in place using a large, decorative overstitch. Alternatively, you could use a large running stitch or, if the patch is in an area that is easily accessible using your sewing machine, you could machine-stitch it in place **(c)**.

c

Tip

Back your patches with felt to give added strength to the fabric and greater control when applying. For hard-wearing areas such as knees, you will still need to use a sturdy top fabric.

Baking Days

Home baking plays an important part in our lives: it's great fun to make cakes, biscuits and bread, particularly if you can get your children involved. Of course, this can be a messy business, so what could be better to keep the flour at bay but these homemade aprons! The adult version is a pretty 1950s-style apron, while the child's version offers more coverage with its practical bib. Harvest has a place close to our hearts and therefore we chose warm, earthy colours and used wheat sheaves and a loaf of bread as motifs to decorate the aprons. As an alternative, you could use cupcake or gingerbread man images like those found in the Party Time project (pages 76–79) combined with bright checks, stripes and denims.

The adult apron has a softly gathered waistband, ties and a simple yet effective faced scalloped edge. It is finished with ric rac, embroidery and a sweet patch pocket that uses a wheat-embroidered table napkin as an appliqué detail. The child's apron is also very simple to make. Its patch pocket is taken from a pair of jeans and is finished with a cottage loaf appliqué (try drawing this freehand, using our image as inspiration).

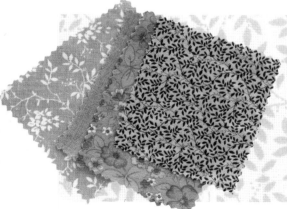

Fabric focus

For the adult apron we used four soft florals in muted colours. Although they are quite different, all the prints are small and each design has a colour that links with the other fabrics to complement the whole. The fabrics should be medium-weight and machine-washable. You could easily add your own appliqué or patterned fabric for the patch pocket detail. For the child's apron, we chose stripes and checks to suggest a traditional chef's apron in blacks and whites.

Adult's apron

You'll need five printed medium-weight cotton fabrics for this project. We used four floral fabrics for the apron itself and one plain fabric in a complementary colour for the pocket.

You will need

- Scalloped edge hem and facing: 80 x 40cm (31½ x 15¾in) medium-weight cotton
- Main body: 80 x 30cm (31½ x 12in) medium-weight cotton
- Ties: 80 x 25cm (31½ x 10in) medium-weight cotton
- Waistband: 50 x 12cm (19¾ x 4¾in) medium-weight cotton
- Pocket: 50 x 22cm (19¾ x 8½in) medium-weight cotton
- Pocket detail: 12 x 12cm (4¾ x 4¾in) piece from an embroidered vintage linen napkin
- Ric rac 1m (39½in)
- Embroidery silks
- Double-sided fusable webbing (Bondaweb)
- Polyester sewing thread

You'll find the pattern for this project on page 116.

One Draft all pattern pieces. Before cutting out your fabrics, lay them roughly in position and change them around until you are satisfied with the final placement. Cut out all the pieces.

Two Take the main front piece and press in both side seams 1cm (³⁄₈in). Press over a further 1cm (³⁄₈in), pin and machine stitch in place keeping close to hem edge. Place front and back of scalloped edge pieces w/s together. Machine stitch between the two balance marks along the scalloped edge. Clip around curves (see page 15). Turn through and press. Press side seams above balance marks in 1cm (³⁄₈in). On underside of scalloped facing, press top hem under 1cm (³⁄₈in). Pin and machine stitch scalloped front piece to bottom hem of main body piece r/s together (refer to the pattern for balance marks). Press seam down. Finally pin and hand-hem the underside facing into position.

Three Sew ric rac down each side of the apron skirt covering stitch line. Now, using one row of hand-sewn running stitch (see page 14), loosely gather the top edge of apron, 5mm (¼in) down, making sure that the gathers are evenly distributed. The final measurement should be 48cm (19in).

Four Turn and press in 1cm (³⁄₈in) at both short ends of the waistband piece. Pin waistband and top gathered edge of apron r/s together and stitch. Press seam up towards the waistband. Turn under 1cm (³⁄₈in) and press long edge of waistband. Press waistband in half along foldline. Pin over to cover first row of stitching and machine topstitch (see page 13) around the entire waistband.

a

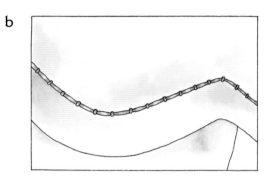

b

Five Press both short ends of each tie in 1cm (³/₈in) and with r/s together stitch along long seam. Turn through (see page 17), press and top stitch around both ties. Measure in 4cm (1¾in) from each end of the waistband. Pin ties into position and top stitch to secure.

Six Draw the pocket detail shape onto the Bondaweb and fuse onto your chosen embroidered napkin. Peel off the backing, position and fuse onto your pocket front and machine appliqué to secure (see page 16). With a contrasting colour of embroidery silk, overstitch to finish. Place front and back pocket r/s together and stitch on seam allowance leaving a gap of 4cm (1¾in) at the bottom edge. Clip, turn, press and close gap with an overstitch. Attach the pocket with a double row of straight stitch (see page 13) **(a)**.

Seven To complete your apron, couch down a length of embroidery thread 2cm (¾in) up from your scalloped edge (as marked on the pattern) with a small overstitch in a complementary colour **(b)**.

The pocket is machine-stitched into place with a double row of straight stitch. The decorative detail of wheatsheaf-embroidered fabric is sewn into place with overstitching in a pink embroidery silk.

Child's apron

This version features a striped skirt and a bib in a contrasting chequered pattern, along with a neck strap and ties round the waist in a smaller check pattern.

You will need

- Skirt piece: 40 x 44cm (15¾ x 17⅜in)
- Bib: 45 x 60cm (17¾ x 23⅝in)
- Neck strap: 45 x 8cm (17¾ x 3⅛in)
- Ties: 60 x 18cm (23⅝ x 7⅛in)
- Patch pocket taken from back of denim jeans
- Scrap of fabric for cottage loaf motif
- Double-sided fusable webbing (Bondaweb)
- Polyester sewing thread
- Fusable interlining (Staflex)

You'll find the pattern for this project on page 117.

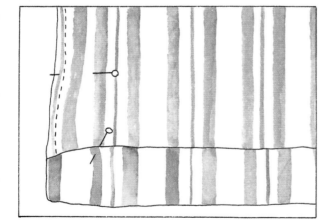

One Draft up the pattern and cut out all fabrics, including the removal of your jeans patch pocket. Draw your cottage loaf appliqué motif onto your Bondaweb. Fuse onto chosen fabric and appliqué onto patch pocket.

Two Press fusable interlining on to w/s of waist and neck straps. To make up ties, press one short end of each tie in 1cm (⅜in) and with r/s together stitch along long seam. Turn through and press. On neck strap fold r/s together along long edge and stitch. Turn through and press.

Three Pin neck strap into position on top bib piece and side straps, as shown on pattern. Place r/s of both bib pieces together and stitch up side seam, across top and down second side seam. Do not stitch the bottom edge. Turn, clip and press **(a)**.

Four Take the skirt piece and press in both side seams 1cm (⅜in). Press over a further 1cm (⅜in), and pin. Turn under skirt hem 1cm (⅜in) and press. Turn under a further 2cm (¾in), pin and topstitch sides and hem **(b)**.

Dad's bread recipe

To make three cob loaves:
1.5kg (3lb 8oz) stoneground flour
25g (1oz) salt
25g (1oz) fresh yeast
1 litre (2 pints) water (slightly warmer than tepid)
70g (2½oz) lard (substitute butter for vegetarians or margarine for vegans)

Dissolve the yeast in the water. Mix the flour, lard and salt together, make a well and pour in half the yeast mixture and slowly start to mix. Add the remaining water and knead well (for about 6–8 minutes). Leave in a warm place to prove. When approximately double in size, knock down and knead for a further 2 minutes. Leave to prove again. When double, mould into 3 round cobs and roll the top of each in rolled oats (a quick brush of water helps it to stick!) To test that it has proved enough, the bread will feel like soft flesh when touched gently.

Bake at 240°C (460°F) for 55 minutes ensuring the tops do not scorch (cover with foil for the last 15 minutes if necessary).

Cool and enjoy sliced thickly with lashings of butter!

Five Place bib bottom edge and skirt top edge w/s together, pin and stitch a 2cm (¾in) seam. Press seams up and trim back excess fabric on bib seam to 5mm (¼in). Press both seams up **(c)**.

Six Turn skirt seam under 5mm (¼in), pin and topstitch. This will create a machine-felled seam.

Seven Finish off by applying patch pocket to the front bib, as marked on your pattern, with two rows of topstitching.

c

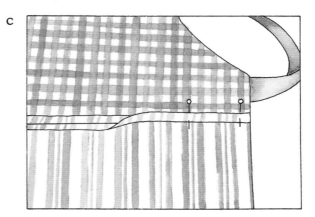

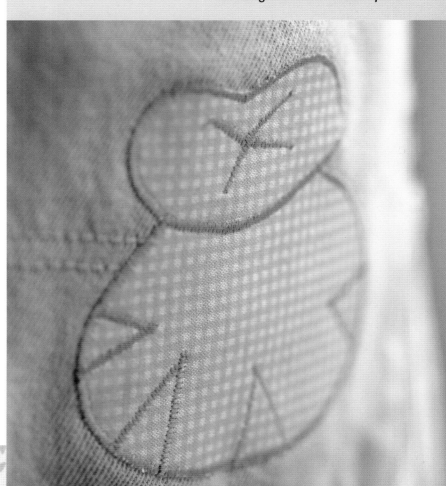

The appliquéd motif of the little cottage loaf adds a charming detail to the child's apron.

Washday Blues

Doing the laundry is one of those chores that a lot of people put off, including us. In fact, Alice often refers to her never-ending washing mountain! We have created this cheerful peg bag to brighten up this mundane task and put some enjoyment back into washday. The peg bag features whimsical details of a washing line with a row of colourful appliquéd clothes made from recycled fabrics. It has a faced oval opening that reveals a pretty patterned lining. Of course, pegging out your washing is also much better for the environment than using a tumble dryer, and you get your reward later when folding up washing that smells of sunshine and fresh air. What could be better than that?

Your peg bag is likely to be left out in all weathers, so make sure the base cloth is durable and pre-shrunk. We used a natural cotton canvas, although coloured canvas, denim or drill would be suitable alternatives. The opening is picked out in running stitch embroidery, and the quirky clothing shapes are machine appliquéd. The bag also incorporates a wooden hanger so that you can hang it from the washing line while pegging out your clothes.

Fabric focus

We made the appliquéd clothing motifs and the contrasting lining fabric from a selection of fresh blue and yellow cottons sourced from old shirts and dresses. Have some fun with this – choose a colour theme, patterns, stripes and polka dots, or even all the colours of the rainbow! If you're lucky enough to have a utility room, you could choose colours that co-ordinate with your décor.

You will need

- 50 x 80cm (19⅝ x 31½in) pre-shrunk natural cotton canvas
- 50 x 40cm (19⅝ x 15¾in) calico or similar lining fabric
- 50 x 40cm (19⅝ x 15¾in) printed medium-weight cotton
- Selection of fabric scraps
- 28cm (11in) wooden wishbone hanger
- Double-sided fusable webbing (Bondaweb)
- Tailor's chalk pencil
- 27cm (10⅝in) garden twine (jute)
- Embroidery threads
- Polyester sewing thread

You'll find the pattern for this project on page 120.

One Draft all pattern pieces – the pattern includes the template and positioning of the oval opening. Using the photograph on page 35 as a guide, design your row of clothing and transfer these shapes onto Bondaweb. Cut out back and front pieces in canvas, one back lining in printed fabric and one front lining in calico. With tailor's chalk, transfer oval opening onto the w/s of the calico lining **(a)**.

Two Pin r/s of front canvas and calico lining together and stitch around your chalk marking. Trim back opening to 1cm (⅜in) and clip (see page 15). Turn through to r/s and press well. With complementary embroidery thread, sew a neat running stitch (approx. 3 stitches to the inch) 5mm (¼in) in from the edge of the oval.

Three Measure down 7cm (2¾in) from opening and, with tailor's chalk, mark a line 25cm (9⅞in). Take the twine and tie a knot in either end. Lay this over your guideline and couch down (see page 19). To create the uprights of the washing line, draw 2 vertical lines in tailor's chalk at either end of your twine (refer to pattern for position). Using brown embroidery thread, stem stitch over marking (see page 18).

a

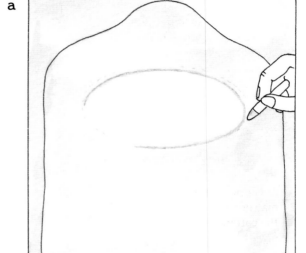

Tip
If you are giving this peg bag as a gift, why not buy some traditional wooden pegs, tie them up with a pretty piece of ribbon and place them in the bag.

Four Taking the Bondaweb clothing shapes, fuse onto your scraps of fabrics and cut out. Position at intervals along the washing line, fuse and machine appliqué (see page 16) **(b)**. Finish off with a long stitch in brown embroidery thread at either end of each garment piece to suggest pegs.

Five Pin w/s printed lining and w/s back canvas together and tack to hold in place. On front and back pieces, zigzag between notch points at hanger opening to neaten. Press to the inside between notches on both pieces and topstitch. Pin r/s of canvas together and stitch 1cm (³⁄₈in) from edge. Don't forget to leave the top open for the hanger! Clip and zigzag over the raw edges to neaten **(c)**.

Six Turn through, press well and insert the wooden hanger. If you are using a different hanger you may need to reshape the top of the pattern to fit snugly.

b
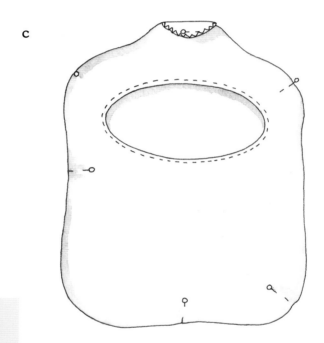

c

Have fun deciding what clothes to make to adorn your washing line. As a fun alternative, why not have a row of coloured socks and stockings?

Keeping Out the Winter Chills

Making wholesome soups and building roaring log fires are some of the joys of the winter season, as is creating a warm and cosy home. If, like us, you live in an old and draughty house, you will really appreciate the need to keep out those winter chills. As the nights draw in, why not settle down to create this beautiful patchwork draught excluder. This is a lovely project to experiment with using the warmer, heavier-weight fabrics from your collection. Introduce plenty of lush texture with woven tweeds, cosy woollens and bobbly bouclés, and have fun arranging a variety of rich, deep sophisticated colours so they complement each other and co-ordinate in the most pleasing way.

This project looks very impressive but is in fact suitable for a beginner. The project features basic patchwork techniques, with pretty embroidered embellishments and button trimmings to add extra-special finishing touches. For a child's room, try a lighter, brighter alternative in the form of a colourful snake in vibrant striped cottons, complete with fabric eyes and tongue and ric rac and button trimmings. Both draught excluders are hollow tubes that are filled with stuffing to make the uniform sausage shape.

Fabric focus

This project is designed to create warmth, so choose from heavier-weight wools, brocades, velvets, scarves and suitings. Remember too that this project is designed to live on the floor and that lighter colours will show up dirt. We used a selection of mossy green and heather coloured bouclés and tweed offcuts. The backing cloth is a dark green wool taken from an old coat. Alternatively, you could use remnants from furnishing fabrics.

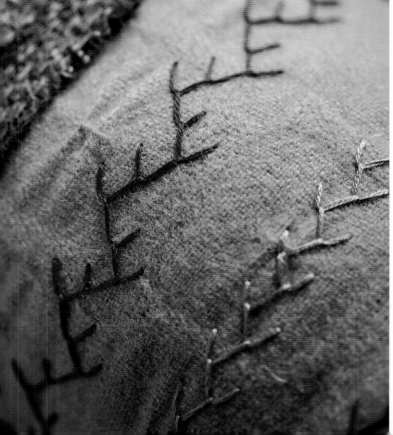

You will need

- Pattern paper
- Selection of woollen fabric pieces or remnants (bouclés, tweeds, tartans)
- Piece of woollen fabric for backing 90 x 22cm (35½ x 8⅝in)
- Embroidery threads

- Selection of buttons
- Polyester sewing thread
- Toy stuffing

Please note that on this project, no pattern is included and therefore measurements given are exact pattern size including 1cm (³⁄₈in) s/a.

One First, on your pattern paper, draft up three templates and label as follows: piece A 12 x 12cm (4¾ x 4¾in), piece B 10 x 22cm (4 x 8⅝in) and piece C 14 x 22cm (5½ x 8⅝in). Next pull out the fabrics you want to use. Place them on a flat surface and rejig until you achieve a good balance. Cut out 6 of piece A, 3 of piece B and 3 of piece C and lay in position. This is a good time to start thinking about the embroidery threads and buttons you might wish to use for the embellishments **(a)**.

Two Take 2 of piece A and fray the edge of one piece **(b)**.

Three Lay this 1cm (³⁄₈in) over r/s of the other piece and sew a machine topstitch in a matching polyester thread to hold seam together **(c)**.

a
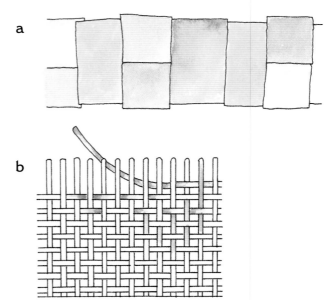

b

c

Tip
Swatches of fabrics are good for sourcing similar and co-ordinating weights and colours. Ask in your local fabric shop for old swatch books.

Four Repeat this method for the remaining A pieces. With the remaining rectangles, sew together using a combination of normal seams (r/s together) and a few overlaid seams. Press all seams flat. Your final patchwork piece should measure 90 x 22cm (35½ x 8⅝in). Add extra or trim as required **(d)**.

Five Now you can have fun embellishing your draught excluder. Make the decorations as simple or as elaborate as you wish. We combined simple embroidery stitches such as running stitch, herringbone stitch, feather stitch, French knots and lazy daisies (see pages 18–19) with some of our favourite decorative buttons. When choosing your threads, pick out colours within the fabrics to create a balance and link them together. You could also add beads or even some braids or trim.

Six To complete the project, pin backing piece and decorated front piece r/s together and machine stitch, leaving an opening of 10cm (4in) in centre of one long edge. Clip corners, turn through and press. Stuff generously, pushing filling well into each corner and ensuring that it is evenly distributed throughout. Close the opening using a small overstitch.

d

The child's version of the draught excluder is made using bold multi-coloured striped cotton fabrics to create a fun snake. We cut the pattern into triangular sections and sewed them together to create diamonds, which we then decorated with ric rac. The snake is sewn up and stuffed in a similar way to the main project, but with the seam running down his centre front. His face and tail have been curved slightly and we have added his tongue, face and spotty cover buttons.

Crafty Curtains

Curtains are a great way to add handmade style to your home. In this project we will show you two easy ways to create fantastic unlined curtains that will give an original look to your windows or doors. A well loved but worn vintage linen curtain was our starting point for the door curtain. We loved the strong floral motifs on the curtains, but they were rather overpowering as a whole. Our solution was to use a neutral hemp base cloth and scatter it with motifs cut out from the original curtain. The addition of some luscious silk doupion made a beautiful decorative border.

Our second project is a pair of fun nautical curtains. We embellished ours with stars, a moon, boats and ric rac ribbon, but you could use any of the motifs in the book or create your own.

Making curtains may seem complicated, but it need not be overwhelming. You may find the most difficult aspect is in coping with the sheer quantity of material, but we give you advice on how to handle larger areas of fabric. This project illustrates how you can use simple machine appliqué to enhance plain shop-bought materials and create something unique.

Fabric focus

When choosing the unlined shop-bought curtains for the base material, a neutral, plain colour is most effective. Choose a base cloth that complements the fabric you are using for the motifs: linen, hemp or velvet would be ideal. We used a range of medium-weight cottons for the nautical motifs; avoid heavier-weight fabrics that may overweigh the base cloth and stick to ones of a similar weight to your curtains.

Door curtain

This project features wonderful contrasts, with the hemp base contrasting against the rich silk doupion borders, and the cut-out motifs adding another layer of texture and colour.

You will need

For a finished door curtain 2.2m (86½in) long:
- 2.24m (88in) base cloth – hemp or heavy-weight linen (union) 140cm (55in) wide
- 2 pieces silk doupion 40cm long x 70cm wide (15¾ x 27½in)
- An old curtain or fabric with a definite motif that can be easily cut around
- Double-sided fusable webbing (Bondaweb)
- Polyester sewing thread
- 140cm (55in) curtain header tape

a

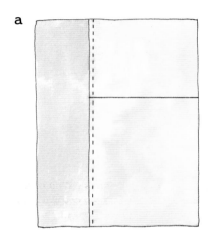

b

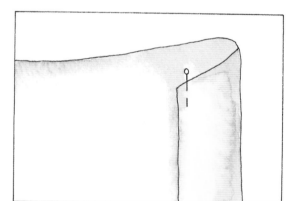

One To create your top and bottom borders, take the two pieces of silk doupion and r/s together sew along the shorter edge and press seam open. This can now be treated as one piece. Cut the doupion into two pieces along the width to measure 17cm (6¾in) deep (top border) and 32cm (12½in) deep (bottom border). If your border fabric is 140cm (55in) wide you can omit the first part of this step.

Two Take the top border and press under one long edge 1cm (⅜in). Place the r/s of the raw edge of the doupion to the w/s of the top edge of the hemp and stitch. Press the doupion to the front so that it lays flat to the hemp and smooth out any wrinkles. Pin along the pressed-under edge and topstitch in position. Repeat on the bottom border **(a)**.

Three Turn under side seams 1cm (⅜in), press and turn under another 1cm (⅜in), mitring each corner (see Party Time project for mitring, pages 76–79). Stitch along the seams **(b)**.

Tip
Motifs cut out from vintage fabrics can also be used as patches. Why not try stitching them onto a cushion cover to complement the curtains?

c

d

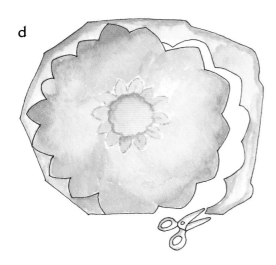

Four Select the motifs from your original curtain (you will need at least 25 depending on their size – fewer if they are very large). Cut roughly round each motif leaving at least 2cm (¾in) excess **(c)**.

Five Cut out Bondaweb to generously cover each motif and fuse to the reverse. Carefully cut around each motif. Position and pin each motif onto the curtain, taking care that they are equally balanced. When satisfied, take the iron and fuse each motif into place **(d)**.

Six Machine appliqué each motif (see page 16) using a complementary polyester thread.

Seven Finally, fold under both raw edges of the header tape 1cm (³⁄₈in) and pin to the top edge of the w/s of the curtain and topstitch all the way round to hold in position.

Here we have stitched our motifs with a complementary machine appliqué stitch, but you could use a darker colour to give a more definite outline, or embellish with beads and hand-embroidered stitch detail.

Nautical curtains

We used a wide selection of spotty, striped and check fabrics taken mostly from a range of blue medium-weight cotton shirts for the boat sails, which stand out crisply against the plain background. The boat and star templates are provided (see page 125), but have a go at drawing your own crescent moon.

You will need

- A pair of unlined ready-made curtains (NB: our curtains are 114cm wide by 138cm drop/45 x 54¼in. You will need to vary these quantities to fit your curtain size)
- 8 different medium-weight cottons 50 x 30cm (19¾ x 12in) in blues for the sails
- 8 different medium-weight cottons scraps in reds for the flags
- 45 x 45cm (17¾ x 17¾in) navy needlecord or similar for the boat bases
- Gold or yellow linen for stars
- Silver satin or similar for moon
- 2m (78¾in) double-sided fusable webbing (Bondaweb)
- Approx 3m (118in) per colour of 5 different ric rac ribbons
- Coloured polyester thread

One First buy a pair of curtains that will fit your chosen window and then plan out your design. Decide how many appliqué boats and stars you wish to have per curtain and in what position (see page 125 for boat and star templates). Trace your boat and star motifs onto the Bondaweb. You will need to reverse the boat and moon patterns for your second curtain, to create a mirror-image. Choose your fabrics and fuse the Bondaweb onto the reverse. Cut out around edges and in between sails and put to one side. We cut all the boat bases from the same fabric and varied the sails and the flags.

Two On a flat surface lay out one of your curtains. Place the cut-out boat base, sails, flags, star and moon pieces into position. Using a tape measure to find the centre point and distance from each side is always helpful when positioning a lot of motifs. Stand back and rejig the pieces if necessary. Aim to achieve a good flow of boats, gently bobbing up and down in the water. When you are happy, loosely pin the pieces into position (a).

Three If you are using ric rac for the waves, now is the time to plan out where you would like it stitched. We measured up at our side seams and started and finished each row of ric rac at the same height. It then curves up and down beneath the boats in a gentle but reasonably symmetrical way. Pin the ric rac well and, using a matching thread, stitch each row in place, turning under at the ends to neaten.

a

Tip
We chose to appliqué boats to create a nautical bedroom feel. Appliquéd flowers in soft printed florals would work equally well for a more feminine room.

Four Lay work down and pin all motifs into their final position. Take your curtain to the ironing board and press each motif under a pressing cloth to fuse in place. Pop a couple of pins in to hold them secure in case they move when machine stitching. As curtains contain a lot of fabric, rolling the bulk of the curtain and stitching in sections makes the fabric easier to control. Machine appliqué (see page 16) each shape into place using a zigzag stitch in a matching thread.

Five Now lay down the completed curtain next to the second curtain and copy as a mirror-image. Use a tape measure for accurate positioning. Repeat steps 2, 3 and 4.

The wavy lengths of ric rac add to the sense of movement and create a feeling of rippling water. A few rows of running stitch would also give the same effect.

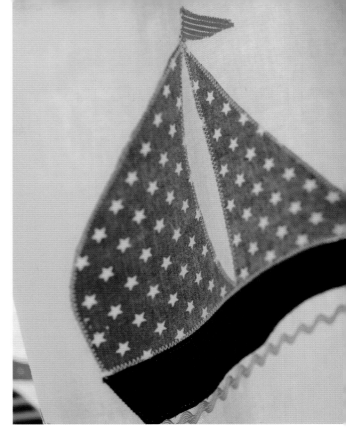

Floral Delights

Making your own floral artworks is a truly delightful recycling project. It makes use of all those small scraps of fabric that you can't bear to throw away, especially beautiful materials such as silks and velvets. We have chosen a golden sunflower to illustrate the technique, but we have also provided alternative templates for the more complex shapes of a poppy, a dog rose and a pansy. These colourful embroidered pictures would make a great Mother's Day present or a gift for a garden lover. To vary the theme, you could make your own designs using fruit or vegetable motifs or create a quirky illustration of teapots and teacups to brighten up your kitchen.

The technique involves simple machine appliqué. It is the heavily beaded embellishment that creates the very sophisticated final look. Whatever theme you decide to illustrate, the secret lies in keeping your design really simple and letting the embellishment do the work for you. In keeping with the recycling theme, we also sourced the pretty gilt frame from a thrift shop. The project instructions explain how to mount your completed design in the frame so it is ready for hanging.

Fabric focus

We used silk taffeta in two colours for our sunflower; we wanted the design to have a rich, opulent look to co-ordinate with the gilt frame. For a more rustic effect, you could use natural cottons combined with a hand-embroidered finish. To create your own floral design, look carefully at the flower noting the main lines and shapes. You need to keep any colour and shading simple – you should only need a maximum of three fabrics.

You will need

· Recycled frame
· 2 scraps of fabric in contrasting yellow silks
· Hemp or natural linen to fit frame plus 4cm (1¾in) extra all around
· Double-sided fusable webbing (Bondaweb)
· Polyester sewing thread
· Embroidery threads
· Selection of gold and bronze seed beads
· Gummed tape
· 2 pieces of thick card to fit snugly inside frame
· Fabric spray mount

You'll find the templates for this project on page 125.

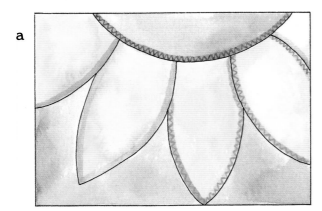

a

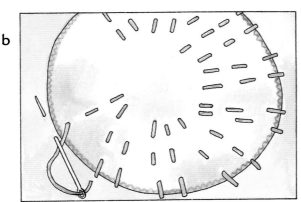

b

One Draft up the sunflower shapes onto your Bondaweb. Fuse, cut out and press onto the centre of your hemp. Machine appliqué each shape (see page 16), stitching right up to the centre circle on each petal. Repeat around the central circle **(a)**.

Two Starting 2cm (¾in) from the centre of the circle, with gold embroidery thread, sew running stitches out from the centre. Stem stitch lines onto each petal to create definition (see page 18) **(b)**.

Three Now heavily encrust your sunflower's centre with your mixture of seed beads. When you have completed the beading, press the underside of the hemp before spraying with fabric spray mount. Making sure that it is positioned centrally, fix to the first piece of the thick card, smoothing out any creases. There should be a 4cm (1¾in) overhang of the hemp all the way around the edge. Take a long length of thread and double it over for extra strength.

Four Fold the hemp over the card and, starting from the middle, work your way outwards lashing either side of the hemp to each other. This helps to keep the finished picture taut **(c)**.

Five Repeat this procedure with the other two sides. Mitre the four corners (see Party Time, pages 76–79) **(d)**.

c

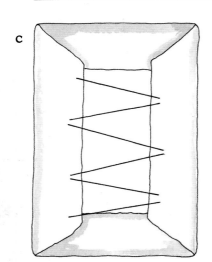

d

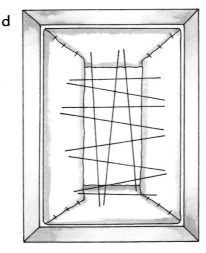

Six Place the mounted picture into the frame and lay the second piece of thick card over the top. Cut four pieces of gummed paper (to measure 3mm/³⁄₁₆in short of the length of the frame). With a wet sponge, dampen the first piece of gummed paper, wipe off any residue and lay over the seam between the underside of the frame and the card. Repeat with the remaining gummed paper around the entire frame and leave to dry **(e)**.

Seven Finally, measure down 10cm (4in) on either side of the frame and insert two eyelet screws. Thread the screws with picture wire or stiff twine and the picture will be ready to hang.

e

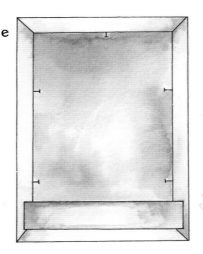

Tip
For a professional finish, define your outlines with machine stitching in a slightly darker thread. Use zigzag stitch if your machine is good, or a straight stitch. Bring out the definition of the floral shapes with beads.

The bead and embroidery details make this project something special. You could easily scale down your motif to make a card, following the steps on pages 84–87.

Out and About

This section focuses on accessories made from recycled or reclaimed fabrics – handy rucksacks, glamorous handbags, little coin purses for your loose change, and pretty flower corsages to brighten up any outfit. Take a bit of beautiful homemade individuality with you wherever you go!

There is immense satisfaction to be gained from recycling old clothes into new, useful items. The rucksacks, in both child and adult sizes (pages 52–57), are a perfect example of this. Old jeans and shirts are given a new lease of life with these handy drawstring bags, finished off with colourful appliquéd motifs.

The little coin purses (pages 58–61) are a great way to showcase all the trimmings that might otherwise languish in your scraps bag. Stitch them onto a base fabric to create a unique pattern – both pretty and practical!

The handbags (pages 62–65) are a lovely way to turn favourite fabrics into beautiful accessories, whether you want one for everyday use or to perfectly complement a special outfit.

Finally, the flower corsages (pages 66–69) are a quick and simple project that will give you the confidence to experiment with pattern and colour. Make lots of variations from all your treasured fabric scraps, give them away as presents, wear them as brooches, or show them off pinned to a favourite bag.

A Walk in the Country

We are lucky enough to live in a beautiful part of the countryside, with some fantastic woodland scenery just on our doorsteps. There's nothing we like better than getting the children out in the fresh air for a nice long walk! We have designed these very practical and sturdy rucksacks with days like these in mind. Just chuck in everything you need, pull the bag closed with the drawstring, and fasten it shut with the toggle closure. The two straps mean you can wear the rucksack on your back and leave your hands free. This project will also give you the immense satisfaction of giving new life to old clothes that you no longer wear. We've decorated the rucksack with a star motif, although any of the motifs in the book could be resized to fit your bag. We've also shown a child's version with a pretty appliqué butterfly (see page 57).

Our bag is made from a pair of taupe denim jeans, with a large navy and white striped cotton shirt for the contrasting flap and straps. This is a fairly technical project involving more advanced sewing skills, and includes appliqué, lining the bag, and making drawstring channels and buttonholes.

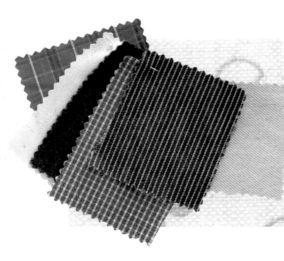

Fabric focus

The fabric for this project needs to be durable, and not have any stretch. We would recommend canvas or heavyweight cotton for the main body of the rucksack and a medium-weight printed cotton for the contrast. You could also use corduroy trousers, coloured jeans or an old printed curtain. We used the back pocket of a pair of jeans for the patch pocket, while the star appliqué is made up of fabric scraps.

You will need

- 1 pair of adult-sized denim jeans, or 60cm (23½in) of canvas or denim fabric 140cm (55in) wide
- 1 extra-large cotton shirt or 1m (39½in) medium-weight printed cotton 112cm (44in) wide
- 2 complementary cotton scraps, 15 x 15cm (6 x 6in) and 10 x 10cm (4 x 4in)
- 60cm (23½in) of calico or similar lining fabric 140cm (55in) wide
- Double-sided fusable webbing (Bondaweb)
- 50cm (19¾in) fusable cotton interfacing (Staflex)
- 14cm (2 x 5½in) lengths of 6mm (³/₁₆in) cotton cord
- 120cm (47¼in) of 4mm (⅛in) cotton cord

- 4 buttons 2cm (¾in) in diameter
- 1 toggle fastener
- 1 decorative wooden toggle
- Polyester sewing thread
- Denim machine needle

Child's version:

Main body, placket and flap as adult version
Cut 2 straps in cotton sheeting or printed cotton 8 x 58cm (3¼ x 22¾in)
Cut 2 drawstrings in cotton sheeting or printed cotton 10 x 34cm (4 x 13½in)
You'll find the pattern for this project on pages 118–119.

One Draft all pattern pieces. Cut along the inside leg seam and open out (w/s together). This will give you a wide surface area with the jean-side seam going down the centre. Remove the back pocket.

Two Pin and cut out main body and side panel pieces. Cut out all contrasting fabric pieces. Your longest piece is the strap; this will need to be seamed. Do this prior to cutting out. Cut out linings and interfacings. Apply the interfacing to w/s of the straps and w/s of one of flap pieces.

Three Trace the double star template onto your Bondaweb. Take your cotton scraps and fuse each star. Position and fuse the small star on to the large star. Apply to the front of the patch pocket using machine appliqué technique (page 16) to neaten all outside edges **(a)**.

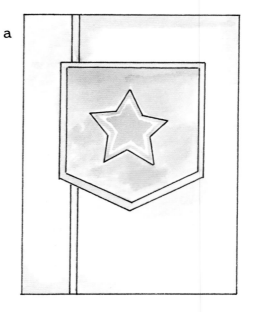

a

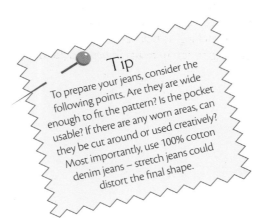

Tip
To prepare your jeans, consider the following points. Are they are wide enough to fit the pattern? Is the pocket usable? If there are any worn areas, can they be cut around or used creatively? Most importantly, use 100% cotton denim jeans – stretch jeans could distort the final shape.

Four Pin the pocket to the front of main body and sew with a double row of topstitching. Take the loop and placket pieces and fold along long edges r/s together. Pin and stitch. Turn through (see page 17) and press. Take the straps. Fold bottom end in 1cm (³/₈in) and press. Fold straps r/s together along long edge. Pin and stitch leaving ends open. Turn through and press. Topstitch all pieces 2mm (⅛in) from edge. Place flap pieces right sides together. Pin and stitch. Clip edges around curve (see page 15). Turn and press.

b

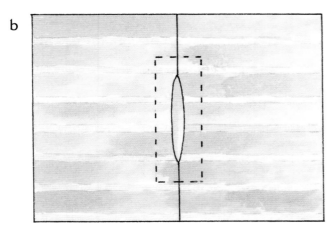

c

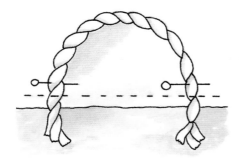

Five Take the drawstring pieces and sew centre front r/s together leaving a gap between the notches. Press the seam open and, from right side, topstitch around the opening 2mm ($\frac{1}{8}$in) from edge **(b)**.

Six With r/s together, pin and sew centre back seam. On r/s of back main piece, along the bottom edge, position the 6mm ($\frac{3}{8}$in) cord at the balance marks as illustrated and stitch in place with 5mm ($\frac{3}{16}$in) seam allowance **(c)**.

Seven Take your side panel pieces, pin r/s together on the bottom seam line and stitch. Press seam open. Pin side panel piece to back main body r/s together with panel side up and stitch **(d)**.

d

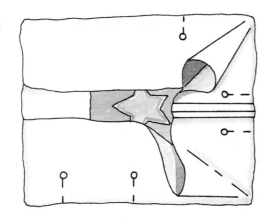

Eight When you reach the corner points you will need to take extra care. At each point, with the needle in the down position, lift presser foot, turn work, drop presser foot and continue.

Nine Repeat process to attach front main body. Clip corners carefully, turn through and press. Make up lining following the same instructions, leaving a 15cm (6in) gap to turn the bag through. With r/s together, pin the drawstring piece to the main bag, matching up balance marks. Remember to place opening at centre front. Stitch and press **(e)**.

e

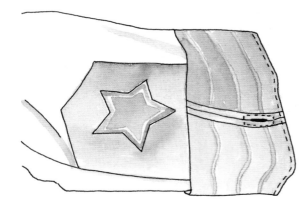

Ten Position, pin and stitch flap piece to back main body (as marked on pattern). Pin and stitch loop piece to strap. Pin onto flap piece 5mm (³/₁₆in) either side of centre back and stitch in place. Finally, pin placket (raw edges pressed under) over all layers and topstitch **(f)**.

f

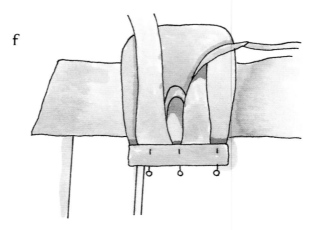

Eleven Turn the main body of the bag inside out and insert lining r/s together, matching at centre points. Pin, stitch and turn through. Press. Close the gap in the lining with a slip stitch. Turn lining back inside the bag, pushing it right down into each corner. Press drawstring over 5cm (2in), pin securely to avoid movement and topstitch 5mm (³/₁₆in) from top and bottom edge to form a channel. Thread the 4mm (¹/₈in) cord through the channel using a safety pin. Push through toggle fastener, tie a knot and fray the ends **(g)**.

g

Finish the bag by making the strap and flap buttonholes as marked on the pattern (see page 17). Sew on buttons and toggle.

Tip
When threading a cord through a channel or toggle fastener, wind a piece of sticky tape round the end to prevent the cord from unravelling.

The child's rucksack is slightly smaller than the adult version; it has fixed straps, no patch pocket and no side panels. The main body is made from a pair of stonewashed jeans and the contrast from a funky pink floral medium-weight cotton taken from a bedsheet. The rucksack has a butterfly motif appliquéd onto the body of the bag and is finished with seed beads. Use the adult main body, flap and placket pattern and the dimensions for the straps and drawstring that are given in the You Will Need list. It can be made up in the same way as the adult rucksack but omitting instructions for patch pocket, side panels, cord loops and adjustable straps. Instead, stitch the straps in position at the balance marks on the bottom seam. For a boy's version, try using an olive-green corduroy with a dark green check contrast and a snail motif.

Loose Change

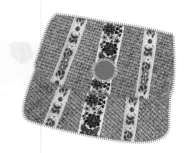

We have designed a little money purse that is ideal for holding all your loose change. Unusual vintage ribbons and trims stitched onto plain linen to form a truly original base cloth was our starting point for this project. When you make your own interpretation, this project is ideal for showcasing your favourite trimmings. The possibilities really are endless, depending on what you have stashed away in your trimmings box. You could use lace, ric rac, strips of fabric, cord, buttons or hand embroidery for these purses. How about trying a patchwork alternative made up of small squares from all the leftovers from your larger projects? You could also use the fabrics from swatch books; these are generally colour-coordinated and make designing a little easier. Just delve into your pile of scraps and have some fun!

The purse is so simple to create that once you have made one you will want to make the project again and again. This is a particularly good starter project for a beginner sewer or for an aspiring designer and one that, with help, an older child could tackle, so have fun combining colours and patterns and be bold with your experiments.

Fabric focus

We used good-quality white linen from a salvaged vintage tablecloth and combined it with retro patterned ribbons to create our distinctive purse. It is fastened with a popper closure and has a retro button sewn on as a decorative finish. The lining fabric is a pretty floral needlecord, taken from an outgrown child's dress. Light-weight or flimsy fabrics will need mounting – plain cotton or calico is best for this.

You will need

- 40 x 20cm (15¾ x 8in) plain linen
- 40 x 20cm (15¾ x 8in) white cotton for mounting
- 40 x 20cm (15¾ x 8in) patterned lining fabric
- Selection of patterned ribbons
- 1 vintage button
- 1 popper/snap fastener
- Fabric spray adhesive
- Polyester sewing thread

You'll find the pattern for this project on page 120.

One Cut out all your fabrics. Using the fabric spray mount, spray the mounting cotton and bond to the w/s of your two top fabric pieces. Lay your chosen ribbons on to the r/s of your front and back purse pieces. Pin and line up the front and the back at the seams and front flap. Re-jig as desired, re-pin and stitch in a contrasting coloured thread **(a)**.

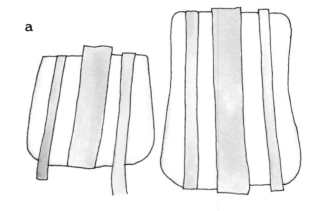

Two Taking your front purse and front lining, place r/s together and stitch the top straight seam. Press the seam up towards the lining and on the lining stitch an understitch 1mm ($^1/_{20}$in) from the edge. This will help the lining to stay in position when the purse is completed **(b)**.

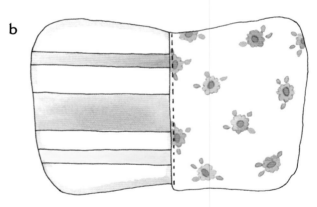

Three Take the back purse and back lining pieces and with r/s together pin at balance marks and around top curved flap only. Stitch. Snip in at balance marks. Trim back the raw edges of the seam to 3mm ($^3/_{16}$in) to reduce bulk. Clip at curves, turn and press **(c)**.

Tip

If you are using a loop and button fastening, cut 14cm (5½in) of thin cord and knot to make a loop. Insert the loop in to the centre top seam of your front purse at step 3 to secure. The best buttons to use with a loop closure are shank buttons. Large beads are also good.

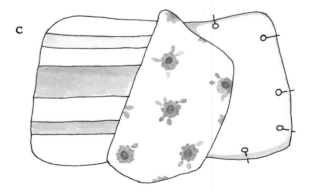

Four Pin r/s of top fabrics together, matching up the bottom curve, and stitch. Double back at each side where the top fabric meets the lining. Push the flap into the main purse and now pin the two lining pieces r/s together, making sure they fit correctly at the bottom. You may think that it doesn't quite fit as there is a little excess on the back lining piece, but you will see later on that when the purse is turned through this excess is needed. Starting 1cm (³⁄₈in) below the excess, stitch around the lining, leaving a 4cm (1¾in) gap on the bottom edge for turning through. Trim back seams and clip. Turn purse through gap, pushing into all the seam edges to make crisp edges, and press well. Close the gap in the lining with an overstitch **(d)**.

Five Press well and sew up using a small overstitch to close the gap in the lining at the side seams. This should now all lie flat. Sew on popper/snap fastener and decorative button.

Heavily embroidered vintage linens create superb little purses. Our variation is complemented with a pink lining and finished with a simple understated loop and button. In complete contrast, the bold red and blue spotty purse shows the effectiveness of simple themed patchwork.

d

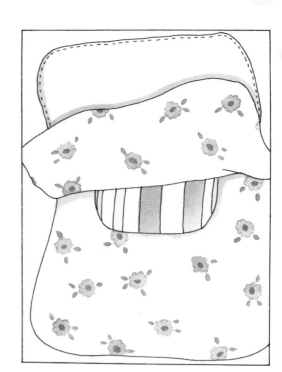

Beautiful Bags

Fabric handbags never go out of fashion and are a wonderful way of accessorizing any outfit. Have you longed to try making one of your own but thought it would be too difficult? Now is the time to try. This bag is easy to construct, doesn't use loads of fabric and the different finishes we show you will make it look sophisticated and original. The bag used to illustrate the steps is made from a checked wool remnant with a silky lining (taken from the skirt used to make Silas the Dog; see pages 102–105), while the handles were taken from a suede jacket. The funky three-dimensional flower is made from the same suede together with a wool scrap. It is finished with a vintage button.

The bag is constructed in two pieces with a seam running across the bottom corners to give it more shape. It can be made with either a satchel-style strap or two shorter handles and can be fastened with a metallic fastener or luxurious silk or satin ribbon. Making this handbag will be great fun; you can really stretch your imagination when embellishing it to create a unique designer bag of your very own.

Fabric focus

This is a versatile project in that most fabrics will be suitable for making this handbag. We used a soft brown and green checked wool combined with real suede to create an everyday bag, but one that could equally well be worn to a wedding or on a special outing. We suggest using precious or funky fabrics that you have had for ages and were just waiting to make something special with.

You will need

- 30 x 80cm (12 x 31½in) checked wool remnant
- 30 x 80cm (12 x 31½in) lining fabric (can be recycled from old clothing)
- 30 x 80cm (12 x 31½in) canvas for interlining
- 15 x 16cm (6 x 6¼in) lining for pocket
- Suede jacket or skirt (not panelled) for handles and decoration
- Scrap of wool for decoration
- 1 large vintage button
- Double-sided fusable webbing (Bondaweb)
- Metallic magnetic clasp fastener
- Fabric spray mount
- Polyester sewing thread
- Pressing cloth

You'll find the pattern for this project on page 121.

One Draft up all pattern pieces and cut out. Draw out your large and small flower motifs onto Bondaweb. You can either draw your own flower shapes freehand or scale up the motifs given for the flower corsages (pages 66–69) to your preferred size. Fuse the larger one onto the suede and the smaller one onto the plain wool. Cut out, peel off paper backing and fuse both flowers onto corresponding fabrics. Zigzag round the edges of both flowers and put to one side.

Two Using the fabric spray mount, spray the canvas and bond to the w/s of front and back pieces. Place small flower on top of large flower and pin to the centre of r/s front bag. Starting at the middle point, using machine straight stitch, sew out approx 3cm (1¼in) into each petal to secure the flower and add decoration.

Three To prepare the inside pocket, turn over the top edge 1cm (³⁄₈in), press and turn over another 1cm (³⁄₈in). Press and topstitch. Zigzag round the remaining three edges to neaten and then press under 1cm (³⁄₈in). Pin into position on back piece of bag lining (see pattern) and sew a double row of topstitch around the three edges to secure **(a)**.

Four To make up the bag and lining, pin r/s front and back pieces together and sew side seams and bottom seam of bag (leave a 10cm/4in gap in the bottom seam of lining to turn bag through). Press seams flat. To create the base for the bag, still working from the w/s, fold the bottom bag corner open along the bottom seam, measure in 3cm (1¼in) and stitch a straight stitch at right angles across the width. Repeat on all corners of both top fabric and lining **(b)**.

Five With r/s together, pin, tack and stitch the top edge of the bag to the top edge of the lining **(c)**.

a
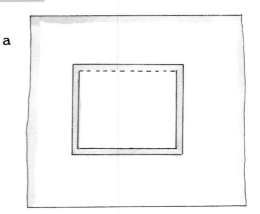

b
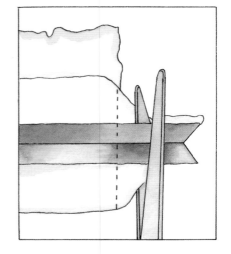

c
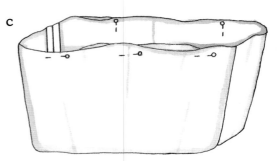

Tip
To avoid the metallic workings of the clasp being visible from the front of the bag, insert a strip of canvas between the fabric and the clasp wings before pushing into place.

Six Turn through to the right side. Press the seams up towards the lining and understitch on the lining side **(d)**.

Seven Push the lining into the bottom corners and press with steam ensuring that you give the sides a crisp edge to create the side panels.

Eight Take the handles and press the long edges under 1cm (³⁄₈in). Pin and topstitch all the way around the edges. Press the short edges under 1cm (³⁄₈in) and pin into position (see pattern). Stitch a 2cm (¾in) square, 1mm (¹⁄₂₀in) from the edge to secure strap and finish with a diagonal stitch row for extra strength. Repeat to secure other three handle edges.

Nine Insert your metallic clasp as per instructions on packet. Slip stitch up the lining and finally sew the vintage button onto the centre of the flower. Give a final steam press.

d

Tip
The funky flower we have used here uses the same motif that appears in the Make Do and Mend and Flower Corsages projects and is sewn onto the bag to give a three-dimensional look. Alternatively, you could use a butterfly motif to appliqué a collection of butterflies onto the front of your bag and even have some positioned along the straps.

Two stunning alternatives to the wool handbag are this beautiful silk devoré evening bag mounted onto pink linen and embellished with complementary beads, and a bold vintage linen furnishing fabric with an appliquéd paisley motif inspired by the pattern.

Flower Corsages

These flower corsages are a novel and attractive way to make use of your favourite fabric scraps. The creative possibilities for these brooches really are endless; they are perfect for showcasing precious and unusual buttons and beads saved from favourite old clothing or thrifted treasures. Colourwise, the sky is the limit. Be bold with your combinations of colours and textures. From pretty florals and funky retros to winter wools and velvets, you could make a corsage to coordinate with every outfit. These corsages look fantastic pinned on to a jacket, but they could also jazz up a hat or a bag.

The principles of making these fun and fashionable brooches are similar to the Make Do and Mend patches (pages 22–25), but take the idea a step further. Felt in a coordinating colour provides a stable backing, and the wadded interlining gives a three-dimensional effect. These brooches would make beautiful gifts and are a simple project for those of all abilities to create.

Fabric focus

Experimenting with varying the thread colour and the fabric type can create a very different feel. You could mix plain red or blue linen with a matching polka-dot fabric, or create a winter flower using offcuts of wool and plaid fabrics in deep, earthy tones. Finish off and embellish the corsage with quirky buttons, pretty beads or a complementary stitch detail.

You will need

- Favourite fabric scraps
- Double-sided fusable webbing (Bondaweb)
- Wadding
- Felt for backing
- Brooch back
- Buttons or bead embellishments
- Polyester sewing thread

You'll find the template for this project on page 125.

You'll find the template for this project on page 125.

Tip

For gift ideas, why not pin your brooch onto the centre of a blank greeting card and send it to a friend? Or, for a great hair accessory, stitch the made-up flower onto a hair elastic.

a

b

c

One Draw up the small and large flower templates onto your Bondaweb. Fuse onto w/s of chosen fabrics and cut out. Peel paper backing off fused fabric flower. Sandwich the wadding between your felt backing (at bottom) and the fabric flower glue side down (at top). Cover with pressing cloth and fuse **(a)**.

Two Cut out roughly around flower shapes and straight stitch slowly through all layers around both flowers 2mm (¹⁄₁₀in) from the edge **(b)**.

Three Trim back wadding and felt to edge of fabric flower. With the zigzag stitch set the same as for machine appliqué, carefully stitch around the large and small flower shapes to finish the edges. Take your time and do not rush this part. After you have stitched around the first petal, continue for a further 3–4mm (³⁄₁₆in). Stop and with the needle in the down position lift the pressure foot, turn just shy of 360 degrees, drop the foot and you will be ready to stitch the next petal. Repeat this process until you have stitched around the entire flower **(c)**.

Four When you have finished both flowers, lay the small flower over the larger flower and stitch through the centres to hold in place. Apply your chosen button or beads at this stage. Finish your brooch by sewing on a metal brooch back with double sewing thread for extra strength.

Tip

Instead of zig-zagging to neaten the flower edges, you could finish by hand with a blanket stitch in a contrasting embroidery thread.

Have fun choosing your fabrics for this project. Embellish with buttons, beads or stitch details to create a huge variety of different effects.

Let's Celebrate

Life is something to celebrate and this section focuses on making handmade items to make your holidays and special occasions even more memorable. Use your sewing skills and your fabric scraps to really celebrate life! Make beautiful gifts for your friends and family, and create special pieces to bring colour and cosiness to your home.

The festive flags (pages 72–75) are a quick and simple project that will instantly cheer up any room or brighten up a festive occasion. Have fun making the colours of the bunting appropriate to the occasion – try fresh spring colours for Easter, or baby blue or pink bunting to celebrate a christening.

The appliquéd tablecloth and napkins (pages 76–79) depicting fabulous party food are just the thing to turn any meal time into a celebration, while the Halloween gift bags (pages 80–83) will soon be filled with seasonal treats. We've offered an Easter version too; you could also create bags with an individual touch for family members' birthdays.

The handmade cards (pages 84–87) and the scented decorations (pages 88–91) are simple but beautiful projects to celebrate special occasions such as birthdays, weddings and Christmas. These items are miniature works of art that are sure to be treasured by their recipients.

Festive Flags

To us, bunting conjures up a nostalgic atmosphere, evoking memories of street parties, summer fêtes and the 1940s and 50s. In this project we've given bunting a revival and brought it right up to date. These festive flags can be used for decorations at a special occasion such as a summer party, or left up every day to brighten up a bedroom. You can choose just about any colour combination you want. Have fun creating your bunting to a theme: you could choose colours to complement a specific interior, or use the colours of your national flag, or you could celebrate a special day such as Halloween (see page 81 for some Halloween motifs). In our variation project (page 75) we've created a more delicate version, perfect for a summer wedding or for a feminine bedroom.

Our flags are double-sided and we have made them out of medium- to heavy-weight cotton shirts in red, white and blue stripes, spots, checks and plain materials. The flags are very easy to create as you basically just cut out the triangular shapes and attach them to the bunting cord, so this would be an ideal project to make with a child for a birthday party or a family celebration.

Fabric focus

For this bunting we used a selection of red, white and blue medium- and heavy-weight cottons in a variety of checks, stripes, plains and spots. Think carefully about where the bunting is going to go: a lighter-weight cotton would be suitable for indoor bunting such as for a child's bedroom, but steer towards heavier-weight fabric with more body for outdoor use as the flags will keep their shape better when the weather is wet and windy.

You will need

- 16 pieces of 40 x 20cm (15¾ x 8in) medium- to heavy-weight cotton fabrics in a variety of colours
- 4m (157in) of 4mm (³/₁₆in) cotton piping cord
- Polyester sewing thread
- Pinking shears

You'll find the pattern for this project on page 117.

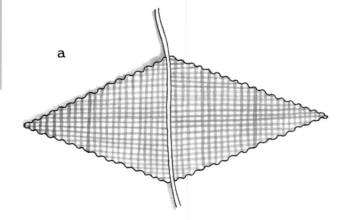

a

One Draft up the pattern and, with pinking shears, cut out and press your fabric selection. We have calculated the measurements as 5 flags to 1m (39½in) with a 4cm (1¾in) gap between each flag. Allow 50cm (19¾in) at each end of the cord to tie the bunting. Open up the flag to the w/s and place the cord on the foldline **(a)**.

Two Close the flag. Pin at the bottom point, lining up the pinked edge, and then pin across the top, close to the cord (you should still be able to move the flags freely along the cord). Repeat for each flag, measuring 4cm (1¾in) between each and then pin through the edge of the flag and cord to keep secure **(b)**.

Tip For heavier-weight wools and decorative bunting the flag pattern can be halved, cut out as a triangular shape and stitched directly onto a ribbon or lace trim.

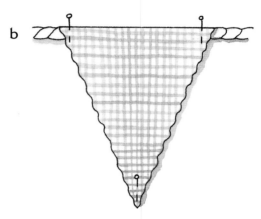

b

Three Starting at the top right-hand edge of the first flag, sew through the cord and down the length of the flag to the bottom point 5mm (¼in) from the edge. With the needle in the down position, lift the foot, turn and sew up to the top left-hand edge.

Four Change to the zipper foot and alter the needle position to the farthest right. Then stitch as near to the cord edge as possible without sewing through the cord. Repeat on each flag and press **(c)**.

Tip As you are sewing your bunting on the machine, fold the excess flags up and pin them together in a pile to avoid getting tangled up.

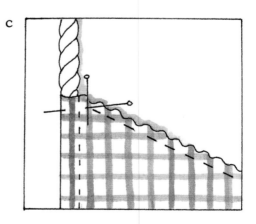

c

Pretty white, pink and cream vintage linens, and embroidered fabrics strung on a length of lace ribbon, make delicate bridal or boudoir bunting. We added a pretty finishing touch with these delicate butterfly and heart motifs.

Party Time

What could be nicer than gathering the children together for a lovely afternoon meal, the table loaded with ham sandwiches, jam tarts, fairy cakes, gingerbread men, blancmange and homemade lemonade? Taking this idea as a theme, we have created some enchanting table linen, appliquéd with party food motifs and finished with vibrant emerald-green ric rac. This will add fun to any meal, whether it is for a special party or every day. You can have lots of fun deciding which fabrics to use to represent your party foods. Just remember that you will want to wash your table linen and therefore choose pre-shrunk and colourfast fabrics.

The tablecloth is made from white linen, pre-washed to allow for shrinkage. It has traditional mitred corners – a sophisticated way to finish off the corners by enclosing all the raw edges. The food motifs use up lots of scraps of fabric and can be as colourful as you like. The four napkins are made using the same techniques but with one appliqué motif picked out on each. This is a moderately difficult project as it involves a lot of fiddly machine appliqué. We wanted to give you the opportunity to have fun designing your own motifs for this project, although you could use any of the templates in the book for an alternative theme.

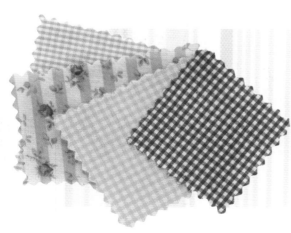

Fabric focus

The fabric scraps that we chose are all loosely based on the colour of the food represented. They include lace for the cake stand, silk doupion for the blancmange, coloured corduroy for the ham sandwich, a small dark orange checked cotton for the gingerbread man, a pretty striped cotton for icing and red and white polka-dot fabric for the cherry on the cupcake.

You will need

- White linen
- 9m (29½ft) ric rac
- Selection of 11 colourful fabric scraps
- Double-sided fusable webbing (Bondaweb)
- Polyester sewing thread
- Pressing cloth

Tip
For a Halloween party you could substitute the food with pumpkin, bat and cat motifs (see pages 80–83). For a summer party, why not appliqué flowers, snails, butterflies and hearts onto the linen.

One To design your motifs for the party table linen, either use ours as inspiration or look through magazines or cookery books for images of your favourite foods. Trace, photocopy or draw these freehand. It is best to keep your shapes simple, using a maximum of four colours for each.

Two Cut out the linen for the tablecloth and the four napkins using the following dimensions:
- 144 x 144cm (56¾ x 56¾in) for the tablecloth
- 37 x 37cm (14½ x 14½in) for the four napkins

Three First construct the tablecloth. Working from the front of your fabric, press under 2cm (¾in) around the entire square. Press under a further 5cm (2in) to create your hem. To mitre the corners, open out pressed seams at corners and, on the 5cm (2in) foldline, insert a pin **(a)**.

Four Make a crease diagonally at this point and score along foldline with your fingernail (pressing with the iron will press out the existing foldlines) **(b)**.

Five Refold the hems and pin into position at mitres and every 5cm (2in) **(c)**.

a
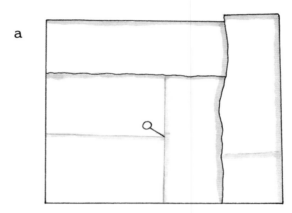

b
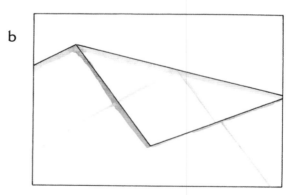

c
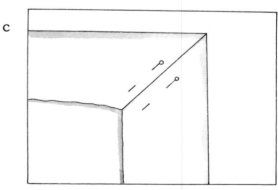

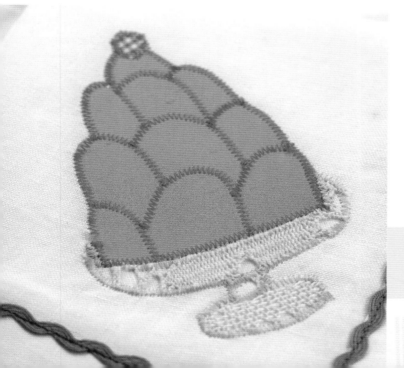

When sewing detail such as on the blancmange, use a chalk pencil to draw the curves first and either machine zigzag or hand embroider, depending on how confident you feel.

Six Topstitch close to the folded edge, taking care at the corners. Slipstitch the mitre into place. Then pin and stitch the ric rac over your stitching line to hide seams **(d)**.

Seven Repeat this process for the napkins, but press under 1cm (³⁄₈in) and then a further 2cm (¾in).

Eight Draw out your motifs onto the Bondaweb, fuse to chosen fabrics and cut out. Take your time positioning the motifs. They need to be at an equal distance from each other and must create an overall balance. When you are happy with their placing, fuse using a pressing cloth to avoid marking the linen. Machine appliqué all the motifs. This will take patience and time, as you need to go around fairly intricate shapes and will need to change threads for each fabric. Work slowly. If you are going round a circle or corner, before lifting the foot, make sure that the needle is in the down position. For the napkin, cut out a single motif of each design (we used a cupcake, a gingerbread man, a sandwich and a blancmange), fuse and machine appliqué diagonally at one corner.

Nine Finish the linen by adding detail to the gingerbread man with bullion stitch (see page 19) in coloured embroidery threads to represent the button mouth and eyes. Press well with steam.

d

Tip
When tackling the machine appliqué, as long as you have a good zigzag stitch on your machine, you can keep the bobbin threaded with ivory thread. If your zigzag is a bit temperamental, you will have to thread all your bobbins with matching thread.

Some of your motifs will need to be fused onto each other to build up the design, such as the cupcake and sandwich.

Time for a Treat

Kids just love to receive presents and treats, whether at Halloween, Easter or Christmas. In this project we show you how to make a generous-sized child's tote bag perfect for Halloween trick or treating. Made in warm autumnal colours from a soft orange wool remnant, they have been lined with a coordinating cotton check from a shirt offcut and decorated with appliquéd jack-o-lantern and cat motifs. These appliqué designs have been picked out with corduroy, silk and checked fabrics in orange and purples to create a rich, seasonal feel.

This project is very easy to achieve. The bag has a simple construction, consisting of the front and back pieces, while the motifs are applied using the machine appliqué technique we've featured in many of the projects. The bag is given some sturdiness with the addition of the contrasting lining and the simple handle. You could make these gift bags for other occasions too; we've shown an Easter variation in fresh-looking colours complete with an appliquéd chick (see page 83). To continue the celebration theme, you could also make some bunting (see pages 72–75) complete with seasonally appropriate motifs.

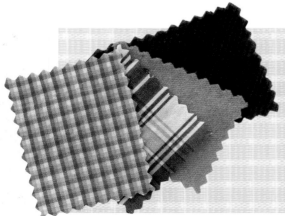

Fabric focus

Most medium-weight fabrics are suitable for this project. They can also be pieced, as illustrated in the Easter variation. You could experiment with mixing plain and patterned designs and coordinating the lining with your top fabrics. Many of the motifs featured in the book could be scaled to fit this bag. Stars or hearts on a printed cotton base would make perfect birthday-party treat bags for boys and girls.

You will need

- Cut 2 pieces for main bag 23cm wide x 25.5cm long (9 x 10in) in top fabric – plain wool or cotton
- Cut 2 pieces for main bag 23cm wide x 25.5cm long (9 x 10in) in lining fabric – cotton checked fabric
- Cut 1 strap 6cm wide x 40cm long (2⅜ x 15¾in) in top fabric – plain wool or cotton
- Cut 1 strap 6cm wide x 40cm long (2⅜ x 15¾in) in lining fabric – cotton checked fabric
- Fabric scraps for appliqué (2 for pumpkin or 1 for cat)
- Double-sided fusable webbing (Bondaweb)
- Black and bright green embroidery thread (for cat motif)
- Polyester sewing thread (purple and orange)

This project does not include a pattern; these measurements are the exact pattern sizes including a 1cm (³⁄₈in) s/a. The templates are on page 125.

One Draft up your pumpkin or cat design onto a piece of Bondaweb (see page 125 for templates). The pumpkin will need two shapes, one with and one without teeth and face cutouts. Fuse onto the w/s of your fabric and cut out. Prepare the pumpkin by fusing cut outs one over the other with the plain background **(a)**.

Two Cut out your bag, lining and straps. Fuse your motif onto the front r/s of your top fabric. Machine appliqué around all raw edges using a matching thread and secure in place. Remember on cat to stitch in leg and neck detail (see template for reference). On pumpkin, stitch around the eyes, nose and teeth.

a

Three To make up the bag, place r/s of top fabric together and sew bottom seam. Repeat on lining. Open seams and press. Place r/s of lining to r/s of main bag and pin both top short seams. Stitch and press. This will create a tube. Fold r/s of top fabric together and r/s of lining together and pin side seams. Stitch side seams leaving a small gap on one side only of the lining for turning through **(b)**.

Four To create the base for the bag, still working from the w/s, fold the bottom bag corner open along the bottom seam. This should make a triangle. Make sure the seams are lined up by pinning through.

b

Five Measure in 2cm (¾in) and stitch a straight stitch at right angles across the width. Repeat on all corners of both top fabric and lining. Turn bag through and press well. Slipstitch opening closed (refer back to step 4 on page 64 for advice).

Six Make up straps by placing r/s of top strap to r/s of lining strap. Stitch together at long edges, turn and press. Topstitch 1mm (¹⁄₂₀in) from edge. With short edges turned under towards lining 1cm (³⁄₈in), pin straps onto main bag 3cm (1¼in) down from top edge at side seams **(c)**.

Seven Stitch a square, 1mm (¹⁄₂₀in) from edge, to secure strap and finish with a diagonal stitch row for extra strength. To complete your treat bag, embroider on all details, using the template as a guide. For the cat, use black and green embroidery thread, and use overstitch for the eyes and black backstitch for the mouth. Now fill your bag with treats!

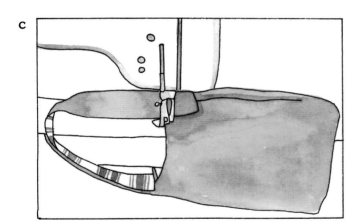

c

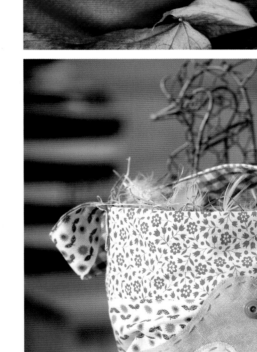

Great for an Easter egg hunt, this variation shows a treat bag made from a patchwork of printed and checked green cottons decorated with a cute appliqué and hand-stitched chick. See page 125 for template.

Creative Cards

A handmade greeting card is a joy to make and a joy to receive. The recipient knows that the giver has created something especially for them, making the card a token to cherish and preserve. These cards are lovely items to keep; they could be framed and displayed permanently. They are very inexpensive to make as you are literally using up all of your fabric scraps. However, the finished effect looks both eye-catching and sophisticated.

We have illustrated the project instructions by showing you how to make a beautiful beaded heart, appliquéd onto linen and hemp. You could use many alternative designs: we have also shown variations for a fairy, a pirate, a sailing boat and a Christmas tree. Any of the other templates in the book could also be used. You could match the colours in your card to a certain theme, for example, using a golden heart to celebrate a golden wedding anniversary. Or you could make cards on a bridal theme – these cards would make great wedding invitations or place settings.

The cards are very simple to make. The motifs are fused onto backing fabric with Bondaweb and then hand-embroidered for a more exclusive, individual look.

Fabric focus

In our main project we used an ever-popular heart image cut out of soft red silk doupion. This is mounted onto an ivory linen square, which in turn is mounted onto a fringed natural hemp. The heart is then hand-embroidered and highlighted with red seed beads to create a precious look. This could be translated into a card for any celebration of love – an important anniversary, a wedding or for Valentine's Day.

You will need

- Red doupion scrap
- 7 x 7cm (2¾ x 2¾in) ivory linen scrap for centre square
- 11 x 11cm (4⅜ x 4⅜in) hemp or natural linen scrap
- 13 x 13cm (5⅛ x 5⅛in) blank white card
- Double-sided fusable webbing (Bondaweb)
- Fabric spray adhesive
- Polyester sewing thread
- Embroidery threads

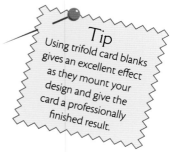

Tip
Using trifold card blanks gives an excellent effect as they mount your design and give the card a professionally finished result.

One Draw a heart and your centre square shape onto the Bondaweb. Fuse and cut out your pieces and press the ivory square onto the centre of your hemp. Machine zigzag to hold in place.

Two Fray the hemp square by roughly 1cm (³⁄₁₆in) all the way round. To do this, pull a thread at a corner edge and remove. Repeat until you reach the desired amount of fraying at the edge and then go onto the next side **(a)**.

Three Fuse the heart onto the centre of the ivory square. Taking a complementary embroidery thread, hand-sew a neat overstitch all the way around the heart **(b)**.

Four Finish by highlighting the centre with evenly spaced red seed beads. Spray the underside of the hemp using the fabric spray mount. Making sure that it is positioned centrally, fix to the front of the blank card. With a natural sewing thread on the top and a white sewing thread in the bobbin, machine straight stitch 2mm (¹⁄₁₀in) from the frayed edge.

a

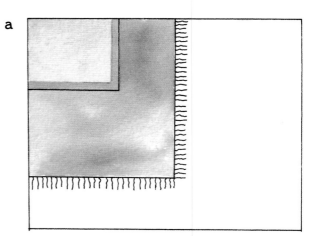

b

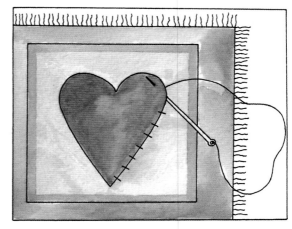

Raid your collection of fabric scraps and turn them into fabulous themed greetings cards for birthdays and other special occasions. You'll find the templates shown here on page 125.

Scent with Love

Scented decorations can be placed in a closet, hung on a Christmas tree, or presented as a gift to a loved one. These items are readily available in shops, but they are so easy to make from your leftover fabric scraps that you really should give them a try. Make them a feast for the senses – not only are ours beautiful to look at and deliciously scented, but we also used lush textural fabrics to make them tactile. The addition of glass beads gives them another individual touch. These decorations would make fabulous wedding favours. Combined with bunting (see the Festive Flag variation, page 75), they would create highly original decorations to help make a wedding day even more memorable.

The project instructions show you how to make a bird-shaped decoration. You could also try making other designs. Remember that the shape will need to work well when stuffed and three-dimensional; strong, graphic shapes such as hearts and stars will work well. The project is fairly straightforward, involving both machine stitching and hand embroidery. We have included some recipes for the scent, although you can of course use or make a scent that you particularly like.

Fabric focus

We used a selection of sumptuous silks, wools and velvets for our decorations. You could also use pretty cotton ginghams and checks for a more rustic feel, or light floral prints for a more feminine touch. For a Valentine's gift, try making a lavender-scented heart made from a delicate cotton blouse mounted onto a soft pink linen and highlighted with buttons and hand embroidery.

You will need

- Two scraps of contrasting fabric for the bird and wing
- 24cm (9½in) 3ply jute gardening twine
- 45cm (17¾in) thin jute twine
- 3 glass beads with 2mm (¹⁄₁₀in) holes to match fabric
- 2 x 5mm (¼in) buttons for eyes
- Double-sided fusable webbing (Bondaweb)
- Polyester sewing thread
- Embroidery threads
- Stuffing
- Christmas scent (see recipe) or dried lavender

You'll find the pattern for this project on page 125.

One Draft up the bird decoration pattern and cut out bird body fabric. Draw the wing shapes onto your Bondaweb. Fuse, cut out and press onto the centre of the bird body. Selecting a complementary embroidery thread, blanket stitch around each wing.

Two Take your length of garden twine, fold it in half and make a knot. R/s together, pin the bird inserting the twine at the balance mark. Machine stitch all the way around, leaving an 8cm (3¹⁄₈in) opening between notches. Take care not to sew over the long strands of twine tucked inside the bird **(a)**.

Three Clip at beak and around curves. Turn the bird through, paying special attention to the points at the tail and beak. Stuff the bird firmly, pushing the stuffing right into the points. Add a teaspoonful of scented mixture inside either side of the stuffing, pin and slipstitch the opening closed.

Four Using a needle with a sharp point and large eye, thread with your length of jute twine. Insert the needle at the bottom of the neck of the bird and pull through the twine so that you have a long length and a shorter length (about 8cm/3¹⁄₈in) **(b)**.

Five Tie a double knot and cut off the excess twine on the shorter length. Thread your 3 beads onto the twine, make a large loop (approx 12cm/4¾in long when doubled) and tie a double knot flush to the beads. Cut off excess twine. Finally, tie a knot in each of the twine legs (approx 3cm/1¼in from body of bird) and trim off the excess twine to approx 1cm/³⁄₈in. Sew a button to both sides of the bird's face for the eyes.

a

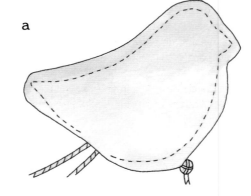

b

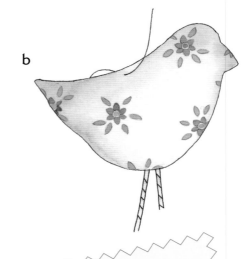

Tip

When turning through any decorations it is important to achieve crisp points. Use a knitting needle or the end of a thin paintbrush to push into the points. Don't be too vigorous, however, or you might make a hole or damage the seam. You can also use these handy tools to push the stuffing into the points.

Christmas scent

You will need:

2 cinnamon sticks
12 cloves
12 black peppercorns
6 green cardamom pods
2 star anise
Dried peel of 1 orange
1tsp orris root powder

You need to prepare the orange part of the recipe at least two weeks ahead, as it needs time to dry out. First peel the orange and place the peel in a paper bag. Put it in an airing cupboard or warm dry place until it has become really hard.

Place all of the spices and peel into a blender and blitz until reduced to a fine powder. Add the orris root powder – this helps to preserve the life of the scent.

This recipe makes a substantial quantity. If you are only making a few decorations, the scent mix could also be put in a bowl with pinecones and cinnamon sticks to make a festive pot pourri.

Lavender scent

The best time to harvest lavender is just before the final flowers have closed. On a dry early morning, after the dew has gone but before the heat of the sun draws out the essential oils, cut the full length of the stems with some sharp secateurs. Bunch them together and tie with string. Place the flower blooms in paper bags in a warm dry place such as your airing cupboard and store them upside down. Check after a week or so and when the lavender has dried, shake off and store in a dark place until needed.

These close-up shots show off the charming detail of the hand-sewn stitches. Use the suggestions above to add scent to the decorations.

Lasting Memories

This section is devoted to projects that can be kept as heirloom pieces and treasured by your family. These items will be particularly meaningful if you make them out of special fabrics, such as cherished pieces of clothing that have been outgrown. The Cushion Full of Memories (pages 110–115) is a beautiful project to showcase such fabrics.

Christmas is a special time for many families, so why not make some stockings personalized with family members' names to bring out every Christmas Eve ready for Santa (pages 94–97)?

Many of us like to keep our children's artworks, so we've come up with an idea to make a more permanent record – turning a child's drawing into motifs to be appliquéd to a cushion or turned into a picture to be framed (pages 98–101). Children grow up very quickly, so we have offered a handmade height chart to record their growth (pages 106–109).

Finally, don't overlook the family pet. We wanted to pay special tribute to a particularly well-loved dog, so we created a project to recreate him in stuffed toy form (pages 102–105)!

Christmas Stockings

Hanging up the stockings is the final touch to Christmas Eve and, certainly in our houses, is something of a tradition. The children can barely conceal their excitement when their own special stocking comes out of the Christmas box and is put out ready in anticipation of Santa's visit. It is very rewarding to create a family heirloom, and these stylish and original stockings can definitely be taken from birth through to adulthood.

Consider where the stockings are going to be hung and whether they will go with the rest of your Christmas décor. Reds, golds and greens will give a very traditional feel. For our girl's stocking, we chose a deep red wool bouclé body with a vintage floral furnishing fabric cuff. For the boy's version, we opted for an olive-green wool body with a wool check cuff.

Making these stockings is fairly simple. The main pieces are machine-stitched together, while the appliquéd motifs are hand-finished with blanket stitch. The stockings are fully lined and have a faux cuff. They are finished off with a hanging loop made from plaited jute twine and, for that special personalized touch, the recipient's name can be appliquéd onto the front.

Fabric focus

Ideal fabrics for this project are wools, velvets, heavy-weight silks and denims. Vintage furnishing fabric is also great as it gives character. Light-weight fabrics can be used, but may need mounting and don't look so luxurious. Carefully consider what colours to use so that they will still be suitable as the child grows up. Lots of little girls love bright pink, for example, but they might prefer something more sophisticated when they are approaching their teens.

You will need

- 80cm (31½in) bouclé or medium-weight wool 140cm (55in) wide
- 30cm (12in) contrasting wool or medium/heavy-weight cotton
- 80cm (31½in) calico or similar lining fabric 140cm (55in) wide
- Scraps for motifs
- Double-sided fusable webbing (Bondaweb)
- 6 strands of 3ply jute twine 50cm (19¾in) long
- Polyester sewing thread
- Embroidery threads
- Pressing cloth

You'll find the pattern for this project on page 120.

One Draft up the pattern and cut out all the pieces. Choose your motif and the fabric you wish to use for it (a colour that is picked up in the cuff fabric, perhaps). If you wish to personalize your stocking with a name, choose your fabric for this at the same time. Draw out your motif in reverse on the Bondaweb and fuse onto w/s fabric. Cut out motif and apply to stocking body. Pick out complementary embroidery threads and blanket stitch around motif.

Two To achieve the lettering for your personalization, choose a font that you like (keep it curvy and bold so that it's easy to interpret in fabric). Type out the name and print it in a font size of around 150 (larger or smaller depending on the number of letters in the name). Hold the paper reverse side up to the daylight, against a window or on a lightbox if you have one, and draw around the letters. This will give you the name in reverse. Draw onto the Bondaweb and repeat the process as for the motif, but use an overstitch to embroider around each letter instead of blanket stitch **(a)**.

Three Pin and sew r/s together, the lining to the cuff and then the cuff to the stocking body. Check your balance marks to ensure that you have sewn the correct pieces to each other. Press seams open. Repeat with other half.

a

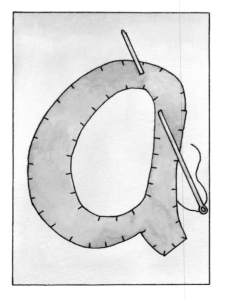

Tip
You could make stockings for each member of the family: choose a piece of your favourite fabric to link them all together and pick out colours within it to create a theme for the stockings.

Four Take your strands of twine and tie a knot in the top end. Keeping the twine taut, using two strands for each section, plait to the end. Fold the plaited length in half and tie a double knot at the loose strand end. This creates your loop.

Five R/s together, pin around the entire stocking inserting the loop with the knot facing outwards at the marker (see cuff pattern). Sew together leaving a 10cm (4in) gap in lining to turn through (see body pattern) **(b)**. Clip at curves and points.

Six Turn through the stocking and press. Sew up the gap in lining with a slipstitch. Push through the lining until you can feel the toe seam of the lining touching the toe seam of the stocking. Push the lining around the inside until it is flush to the seams. Give the stocking a final press.

b

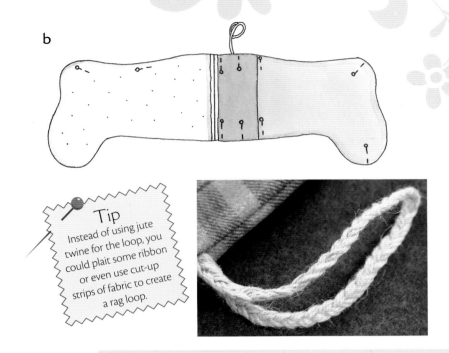

Tip
Instead of using jute twine for the loop, you could plait some ribbon or even use cut-up strips of fabric to create a rag loop.

The edges of the star and heart motifs are picked out in blanket stitch worked in embroidery thread. You can personalize the stocking with the family member's name if desired – see step 2.

Heirloom Artworks

One of our children had a favourite teacher who was leaving to get married. He wanted to make her something really special to say goodbye. He drew a beautiful picture of the two of them skipping along hand in hand on a flower-strewn hill, underneath a colourful rainbow surrounded by hearts. We then interpreted his drawing by simplifying the shapes and choosing lots of colourful fabrics to appliqué the design onto a cushion, finishing it with hand embroidery. As you can imagine, his teacher was delighted with this very personal and thoughtful handmade gift. For this project, we've used another artwork, featuring lots of heart motifs and pretty scrolling lines.

A lot of us keep our children's early drawings, particularly the first scribbles, but this project is a really special way to preserve your child's artwork. We have given you two ideas for this project: to make a framed picture or to make a cushion. This is a fairly straightforward design and would make a lovely first sewing project for you and your child to enjoy together. They will feel much more involved if they have drawn the design that is then made up, so this is a great way to stimulate your child's creativity and imagination.

Fabric focus

Any fabrics are suitable for this project: just look at the design and rummage through your fabric hoards until you find something that matches the colours. It could be patterned or plain, cotton or wool – the important thing is to involve your child and let him or her make the decisions. Choose a plain backing fabric to fuse your design onto; a linen or a medium-weight cotton would be ideal.

You will need

- A child's drawing
- Lots of colourful scraps of fabric (printed and plain)
- Tracing paper
- Double-sided fusable webbing (Bondaweb)
- A4 (8¼ x 11¾in) picture frame or 30 x 30cm (12 x 12in) cushion pad
- Fabric spray adhesive
- Polyester sewing thread
- Black topstitching thread
- Embroidery threads
- Pressing cloth

One Sit your child down with a piece of A4 (8¼ x 11¾in) paper and lots of colouring pens. See what they come up with of their own accord, but if they're struggling, give them some basic ideas such as a flower, a butterfly, a rocket, a snail or a rainbow. Encourage them to keep the drawing simple, bold and colourful, remember that the more complicated it becomes, the harder it will be to adapt.

Two Look at the finished drawing and decide whether it needs to be simplified. You may need to fatten out some of the shapes and break the design down into key colours. Using your tracing paper, draw round the outline of each shape. Turn the tracing paper over and retrace the outline (this will give you the design in reverse). Draft up your Bondaweb by laying over the tracing paper. Choose the fabrics you wish to use on the picture and then fuse the Bondaweb onto the reverse side. Cut out and position onto the backing fabric using the design as reference. When you are satisfied, fuse the fabrics down.

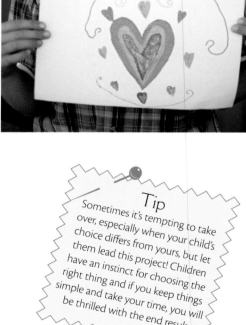

Tip
Sometimes it's tempting to take over, especially when your child's choice differs from yours, but let them lead this project! Children have an instinct for choosing the right thing and if you keep things simple and take your time, you will be thrilled with the end result.

In this variation, we decided to turn a child's colourful drawing of a space rocket into an equally colourful framed artwork.

Three You can either machine appliqué or hand-embroider to finish off your fabric shapes. If you decide to hand-embroider, keep the stitches easy, such as running stitch or overstitch.

Four Depending on whether you wish your finished design to be a cushion or a picture, follow the instructions for making up a cushion in a Cushion Full of Memories (pages 110–115) or framing a finished picture in Floral Delights (pages 46–49).

To make your picture or cushion even more special, encourage the child to write a message on paper. Trace the lettering onto Stitch and Tear (see page 11) and, using a complementary sewing thread, embroider a backstitch over the lettering. When complete, rip off the Stitch and Tear and you are left with your child's handwriting.

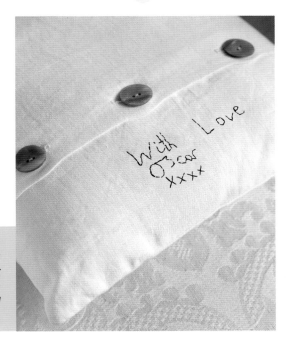

Silas the Dog

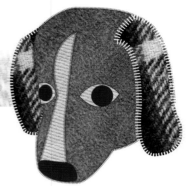

We love our dog Silas, an English Springer spaniel, and we couldn't resist introducing him to you too. Inspired by a 1960s sewing pattern, we have created our very own Silas-style stuffed toy dog for you to make, complete with floppy ears, waggly tail and a very smart leather collar trimmed with buttons. Silas's coat is made from a beautiful-quality woollen skirt sourced from a thrift shop (we didn't have the heart to tell the shop assistant that we were going to cut it up) and a checked wool remnant.

This is a project that an older child could enjoy tackling, with lots of help and encouragement from an adult. The project covers the basic sewing construction and stuffing of a soft toy. There are quite a lot of pieces to cut out, and quite a few steps to the process, but it will be worth it. Silas could be made entirely by hand or, as we have, using a sewing machine. All the patches that form Silas's markings, and details such as his eyes, mouth and paws, are hand-stitched on once the main form of the dog has been made up and filled with toy stuffing.

Fabric focus
We chose soft cream and brown fabrics to represent Silas's actual colours. We used warm woollen fabrics for a snuggly, tactile feel. Suede or felt is ideal for his features, as it does not fray. You could make the whole dog in felt if you wish or, for a fun and colourful alternative, use some funky retro floral cottons (1970s bed linen is a good source).

You will need

- Approx 100 x 60cm (39½ x 23½in) medium-weight plain wool (skirt or blanket)
- Approx 60 x 60cm (23½ x 23½in) medium-weight tweed or tartan wool
- Scraps of white and brown felt or suede for dog's face
- Strip of leather or suede for dog's collar
- Selection of buttons (approx 11)
- Toy stuffing
- Embroidery thread
- Polyester thread

You'll find the pattern for this project on page 122.

a

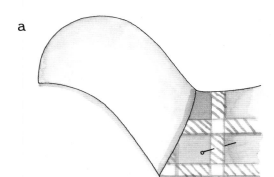

One Draft up and cut out all your pattern pieces. Ensure that you transfer all markings and labels carefully, as this is vital to the construction. Take one of the bottom tail pieces r/s up and lay over one top tail piece, r/s up. Pin and stitch 5mm (¼in) from the seam edge to hold in place. Repeat with other tail piece **(a)**.

Two Neaten seam with hand-embroidered overstitch. Place r/s together and stitch around tail leaving opening at top. Clip, turn through and stuff firmly. Stitch opening closed **(b)**.

b

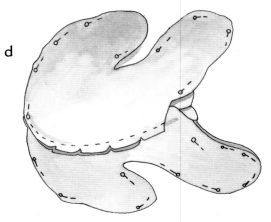

Three Place r/s of top ear and underside ear pieces together and stitch along top straight edge. Trim seam to 3mm (³/₁₆in), press open and bringing w/s together, press and pin. Using embroidery thread, blanket stitch around ear to hold the two pieces together. Repeat with other ear. Pin tail into position on one main body piece at balance marks, making sure the tail curves down **(c)**. Take other main body piece and with r/s together stitch from point C to point D. Clip seams at curves.

Four Take both underside body pieces and with r/s together sew from A to B, leaving an opening between the two balance marks. This is where the dog will be stuffed later. Clip seams at curves. To make up the body, now join the main and undersides pieces together by matching up points B to D and E to F. Starting and finishing at where point E meets point F, pin, tacking if necessary, and stitch, taking care at tail point to match up the seams. Finally, clip all curved seams **(d)**.

c

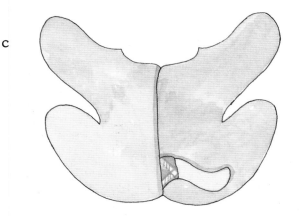

d

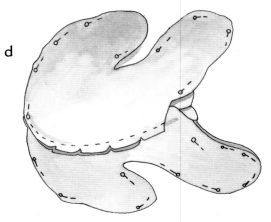

104   Silas the Dog

e

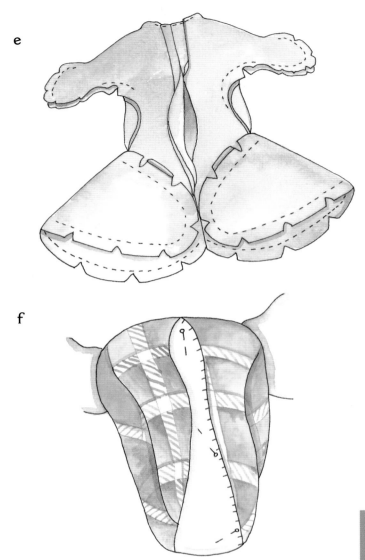

f

Five To make up Silas's head, take head gusset and one head piece. Place r/s together and pin, carefully matching up front to front neck and back to back neck. Gently ease and hand tack to hold. Machine stitch to secure. Repeat with the second head piece. Clip all curved seams. Turn and press. Now attach the head to the main body. Drop turned-through head into main body piece (still showing w/s out). Pin with r/s together, matching up A to A (at front) and C to C (at back). Stitch on the long arm of your machine if you have one. (This is rather like sewing a set-in sleeve.) Clip and turn through opening in the underside seam **(e)**. Stuff firmly – if you skimp on the stuffing Silas will be too floppy. Close the opening with a small neat overstitch.

Six Pin patch and nose pieces onto your stuffed dog (refer to pattern for positioning) and hold in place with a 2mm (¹⁄₁₀in) decorative overstitch **(f)**.

Seven Apply the black centre eye to the white outer eye in the same way. Pin and fix into place with a small overstitch and stem stitch in brown to define eye outline. Stem stitch paw and mouth details. Sew ears into position with a small blanket stitch.

Eight Complete your Silas by making up his collar. Stitch on buttons at 2cm (¾in) intervals along the suede and loosely secure around his neck. To finish, sew a button over the join.

Silas's nose and patches are held in place with overstitch, while his eyes are fixed with overstitch and defined by stem stitch.

As Tall as a House

A height chart is a lovely way of recording your children's growing-up years, and this one can be passed down through the generations to document each new addition to the family. We used vintage fabrics for our height chart to give it a very special look, including ticking to create a clapboard effect to the house and 1950s and 60s furnishing fabrics for the tree. To make this project really meaningful, use clothing or fabrics that recall a certain memory or hold sentimental value so that this is both personal and an heirloom in the making.

We used a series of simple geometric shapes machine appliquéd to give a patchwork effect. The wall hanging is then quilted to give added dimension and finished with a soft suede cat sitting regally at the top window. To record the children's height, we suggest that you choose a different colour embroidery thread for each child and either mark it with a symbol such as a star or heart or, if you are more technically proficient, embroider the child's age against the height scale. The height scale we have used is in feet and inches, but it could easily be converted to metres and centimetres.

Fabric focus

You can choose any fabrics for this project, although printed cotton florals, stripes and checks will work particularly well. The key to the success of this project is combining your fabrics so that there is at least one colour that consistently runs through all of them – in our case, we used petrol blue, green and rose red. Why not try an aqua and pastel colour palette to create a New England look? For the cat use a tactile fabric such as suede, wool or velvet.

You will need

- 122 x 46cm (48 x 18in) of calico*
- 124 x 48cm (49 x 19in) of 50g (2oz) wadding*
- 130 x 54cm (51 x 21¼in) gingham for backing*
- 15 x 84cm (6 x 33in) black and white ticking for house*
- 44 x 10cm (17¼ x 4in) floral medium-weight cotton for garden*
- 3 x 40cm (15¾in) different green floral medium-weight cottons for tree
- 20cm (8in) red check medium-weight cotton for roof
- Scrap of red cotton for chimney
- Scrap of plain brown cotton for path and tree trunk
- Scrap of petrol-blue corduroy for door
- Scrap of small blue check cotton for windows
- Scrap of plain light blue cotton for top window
- Scrap of black suede for cat
- Double-sided fusable webbing (Bondaweb)
- Fabric spray adhesive
- Polyester sewing thread
- Black topstitching thread
- Embroidery threads
- 3 brass curtain rings
- Pressing cloth

You'll find the pattern for some of the pieces on page 124. Otherwise, * indicates exact measurements.

One Cut out your backing fabric, wadding and calico. Draft up all pattern pieces onto the Bondaweb, including the garden and house (see dimensions in You Will Need), fuse onto the w/s of your fabric and cut out. Place each fabric piece into position on the calico (see pattern) and, when satisfied, fuse. As the pieces in this project are quite large, rather than struggling at your ironing board, lay some clean old towels or blankets on a large table top and use these as a giant ironing board.

Two Machine appliqué around each shape in a complementary sewing thread. Press. Using the fabric spray adhesive, spray the wadding and sandwich between the height chart and backing fabric. Stay stitch with a small running stitch around outside edge just within your 1cm (³⁄₈in) s/a using an ivory thread.

Three Quilt the height chart by using a black topstitching thread (this is stronger than regular sewing thread and doesn't tangle so much). Use an even running stitch approx. 3 stitches to the inch. You want the stitches to be obvious as it is part of the overall look. Stitch around each of the shapes to quilt into position. Keep the work as flat as possible while completing this stage. A frame isn't really necessary, but you should sit at a table. You will notice that when this process is completed, it really makes the height chart come alive **(a)**.

a

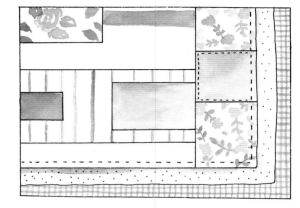

b

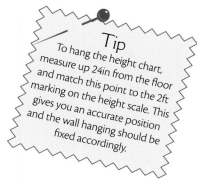

Tip
To hang the height chart, measure up 24in from the floor and match this point to the 2ft marking on the height scale. This gives you an accurate position and the wall hanging should be fixed accordingly.

Four Backstitch across the windows to suggest windowpanes and sew a button on the door to create a handle. Stitch your house number onto the door for a personal touch **(b)**.

Five Measuring 2cm (¾in) out from the edge of the basting line, trim back any excess wadding **(c)**.

Six Press the gingham under 1cm (³⁄₈in) and then turn over 2cm (¾in). Starting from the centre and working outwards, pin every 4cm (1¾in) just within the basting line. Leave the corners until the edges are pinned **(d)**.

Seven To complete each corner, pin one edge in place, turn over the other edge and pin down. Continue around in a clockwise direction, pinning each corner. Slowly stitch the border in place stitching 2mm (¹⁄₁₀in) in from the pinned edge. Keep all layers taut as you stitch to avoid puckering. Slipstitch the openings at each corner edges closed **(e)**.

Eight Using the height scale guide (page 124), take a length of black embroidery thread and backstitch a 2cm (¾in)-long horizontal line at each 12in to mark a foot and embroider the corresponding number – that is, 2ft, 3ft, 4ft and so on. You can mark each inch in between with a 1cm (³⁄₈in)-long line of backstitch.

Nine Evenly space the curtain rings at the top edge of the back of the wall hanging and sew in place with a buttonhole stitch. Gently press.

c
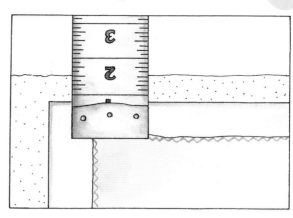

d
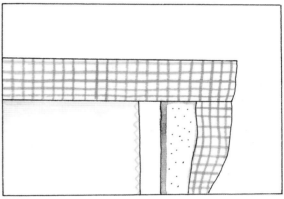

e
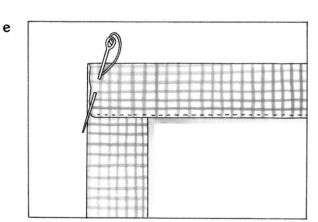

The little detail of the cat sitting calmly in the window was made from a scrap from a black suede skirt.

A Cushion Full of Memories

This delightful cushion gives you the opportunity to use precious fabrics or perhaps baby clothes and dresses that you can't bear to part with as they hold such great sentimental value. We used twelve of our prettiest floral cottons to create a patchwork cushion featuring an intricately appliquéd fairy that would be cherished by any little girl. We used an embroidered blouse for the fairy's dress and gold lamé for her wings. You could use a particularly treasured fabric for the dress with maybe tiny polka-dot or silky fabric for the wings. We found a gorgeous embroidered tablecloth to use for the backing and picked out the lazy daisy detail to embroider on the covered buttons. Alternatively, plain linen in a complementary fabric would work equally well.

This project covers basic patchwork and simple quilting. The appliqué techniques used to create the fairy are more complicated than the other projects in the book and therefore require more advanced sewing skills. As a quirky alternative for a boy, we made up a cushion featuring a jaunty pirate (see page 125 for template). Many of the motifs in the book would translate well for this project, or you could have fun creating your own designs.

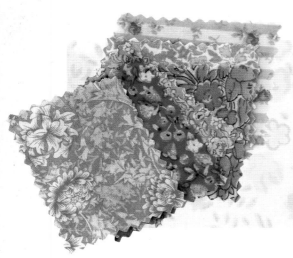

Fabric focus

We used a combination of pretty floral fabrics in cottons for this delightful cushion. When selecting the fabrics, we kept the floral prints small so that they are not overpowering, and chose the colours of the rainbow as a theme. If your child loves a particular colour or you want the cushion to fit into an existing design scheme, you could base all of your fabrics around shades and tones – for example, pinks and reds or lilacs and purples.

You will need

- 17 x 17cm (6¾ x 6¾in) each of 12 floral dress-weight cottons for small patchwork squares
- 32 x 32cm (12½ x 12½in) natural-coloured plain linen for centre
- Embroidered fabric for fairy's dress
- Brown fabric for fairy's hair
- Flesh-coloured fabric for fairy's face, feet and arms
- Gold fabric for fairy's wings
- Embroidery threads
- 62 x 62cm (24½ x 24½in) polyester wadding or batting
- 1m (39¼in) of 140cm (55in) wide cotton calico lining or similar
- 3 x 2.5cm (1in) cover buttons
- Embroidered tablecloth or linen for cushion backing
- 60 x 60cm (23⅝ x 23⅝in) cushion pad
- Double-sided fusable webbing (Bondaweb)
- Fabric spray adhesive
- Polyester sewing thread
- Pressing cloth

You'll find the pattern for this project on page 123
The template for the fairy is on page 125.

One First take the pieces of fabric you wish to use for your patchwork and position these around your central linen square. Play around with them until you are happy with their positioning. Remember to balance stronger colours opposite each other to avoid one section of the cushion looking too heavy. You can adopt a random feel or can link colours with one leading gradually into the next. When you have achieved your desired balance, cut out the 12 patchwork squares and lay in position with r/s up. Starting with the top left square as number 1, work round clockwise and with tailor's chalk on the reverse number all your squares from 1 to 12 **(a)**.

Two Sew with r/s together 2 to 3 and 9 to 8. Press seams open and, with r/s together, place piece 2/3 to top of large centre square and piece 9/8 to bottom and stitch. Press all seams. Now sew side patchwork strips: 1, 12, 11, 10 and 4, 5, 6, 7. Press all seams and with r/s facing pin carefully to central square, matching up corner points and stitch into place. Press and turn to right side.

Three Draft up the fairy template onto Bondaweb. Fuse onto the w/s of your chosen fabrics and cut out. Peel off backing paper and position onto the centre of your linen square. Measuring across to find the centre point will help with a balanced positioning **(b)**.

a

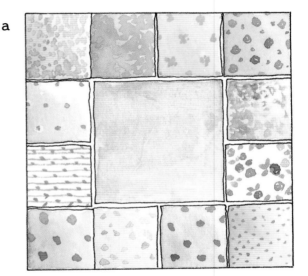

b

Tip
When sewing your cushion up, by starting 5cm (2in) in from one corner, the fabric can be eased in, which will help you avoid unsightly puckering.

Four Machine appliqué carefully around edges with a matching polyester sewing thread. Add the zigzag headdress, dress and wing details (see photo). Cut wadding and wadding backing calico. Using the fabric spray adhesive, spray the wadding and sandwich between the cushion front and calico backing. Stay stitch with a small running stitch around outside edge just within your 1cm (^{3}/$_8$in) s/a.

Five With a contrasting embroidery thread, sew an even running stitch 2mm (^{1}/$_{10}$in) inside of the linen square. Embroider the scattered stars in your chosen colours and finally embroider a star at the centre of the fairy's hairband. To make embroidered stars, first sew a long cross stitch and then diagonally over the top of this make a smaller cross stitch (see photo).

Six Cut cushion backs and calico facings. With r/s together, stitch fabric under flap to calico facing under flap along long edge. Repeat with overflap pieces. Press and turn with w/s together. Mark button positions on overflap. Make buttonholes.

Seven To sew up the cushion with r/s of cushion front facing you (fairy right way up), place over top cushion back (with buttonholes) and pin raw edges to top seam. Then lay over the under flap (without buttonholes) and pin raw edges to bottom seam. All right sides should be enclosed. Pin round all seams and stitch on seam allowance, remembering to double back at the sides where the backing flaps meet to strengthen this potentially weak point. Clip corners and neaten with a wide zigzag stitch (machine set to 4 width and 3 length). Clip corners, turn through flap opening and give a final press.

If the fine machine appliqué seems a little daunting don't forget you can always hand-stitch your fairy instead.

The reverse of your cushion needn't be plain. We used a beautiful linen tablecloth to complement the floral theme of our fairy cushion. It is finished with covered buttons embroidered with lazy daisies highlighted from the fabric.

The pirate cushion is based on a nautical theme, with a combination of reds, blues and greens taken from a selection of checked and striped shirts. The backing is made from strips of three different coloured denims from salvaged jeans. The nautical-style old gold buttons embossed with an anchor made the perfect finishing touch.

c

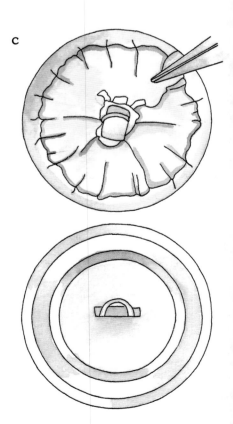

Eight To make the cover buttons, cut 3 circles, 6cm (2³⁄₈in) in diameter, in a plain offcut from your embroidered backing fabric. With the w/s facing you, centre the metal cover button on top. Gently, with the point of some embroidery scissors, fold in the fabric securing into the teeth grips on the underside of your button. Snap on cover button back and embroider a lazy daisy onto the front. Attach your cover buttons to the under flap. Refer to pattern for positioning **(c)**.

Tip
If you were making a cushion for an anniversary present or special occasion, you could ask members of the family to donate a fabric that is special to them to create a very personal and memorable gift that could easily become an heirloom.

Patterns

On the next few pages you will find the patterns for the projects featured in the book, while on page 125 you'll find the motif templates. See page 12 for advice on scaling up patterns and templates.

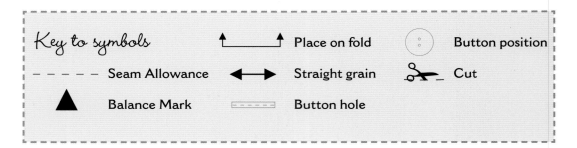

Key to symbols

– – – – – Seam Allowance

▲ Balance Mark

Place on fold

Straight grain

Button hole

Button position

Cut

Baking Days, pages 26–31
Adult's apron – enlarge all by 400%

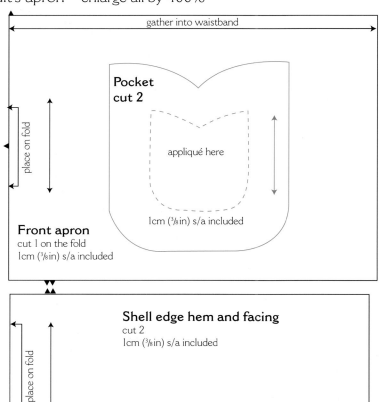

gather into waistband

place on fold

Pocket
cut 2

appliqué here

1cm (³⁄₈in) s/a included

Front apron
cut 1 on the fold
1cm (³⁄₈in) s/a included

Shell edge hem and facing
cut 2
1cm (³⁄₈in) s/a included

place on fold

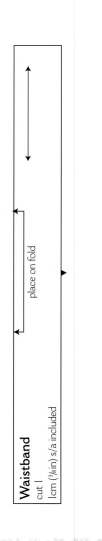

place on fold

Waistband
cut 1
1cm (³⁄₈in) s/a included

place on fold

Waist ties (straps)
cut 2
1cm (³⁄₈in) s/a included

Child's apron – enlarge all by 400%

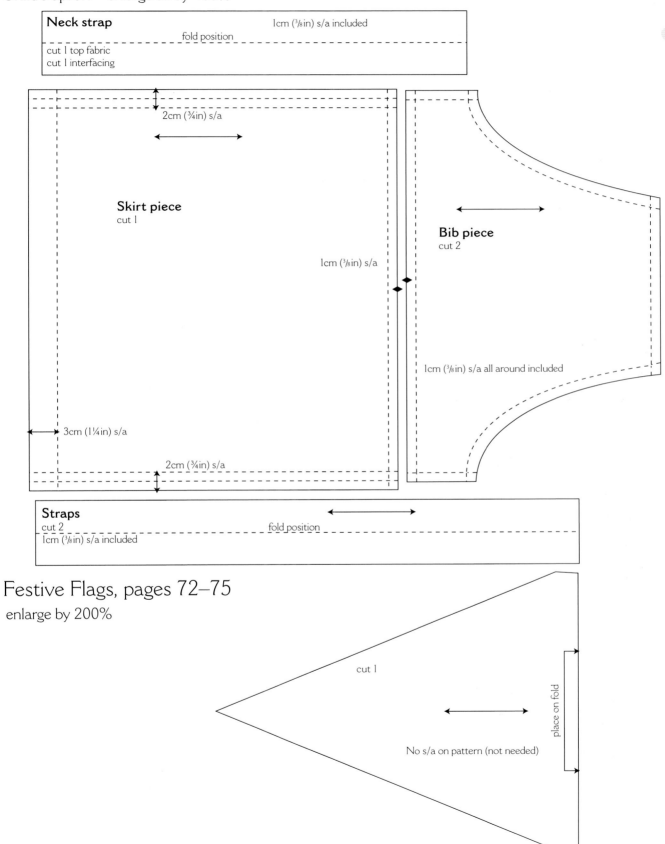

Neck strap
1cm (³⁄₈in) s/a included
fold position

cut 1 top fabric
cut 1 interfacing

2cm (¾in) s/a

Skirt piece
cut 1

1cm (³⁄₈in) s/a

Bib piece
cut 2

1cm (³⁄₈in) s/a all around included

3cm (1¼in) s/a

2cm (¾in) s/a

Straps
cut 2
fold position
1cm (³⁄₈in) s/a included

Festive Flags, pages 72–75

enlarge by 200%

cut 1

place on fold

No s/a on pattern (not needed)

A Walk in the Country, pages 52–57
enlarge all by 200%

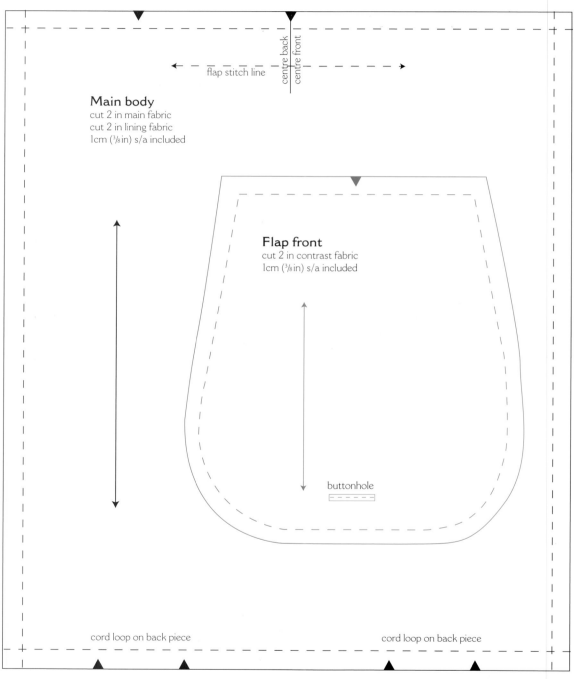

flap stitch line

centre back
centre front

Main body
cut 2 in main fabric
cut 2 in lining fabric
1cm (³⁄₈in) s/a included

Flap front
cut 2 in contrast fabric
1cm (³⁄₈in) s/a included

buttonhole

cord loop on back piece

cord loop on back piece

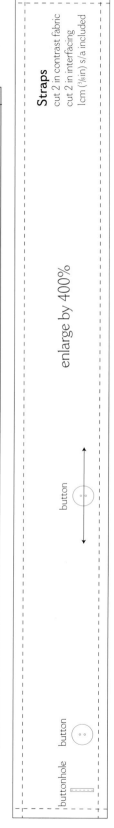

Straps
cut 2 in contrast fabric
cut 2 in interfacing
1cm (³⁄₈in) s/a included

enlarge by 400%

button

button

buttonhole

A Walk in the Country continued...
enlarge all by 200%

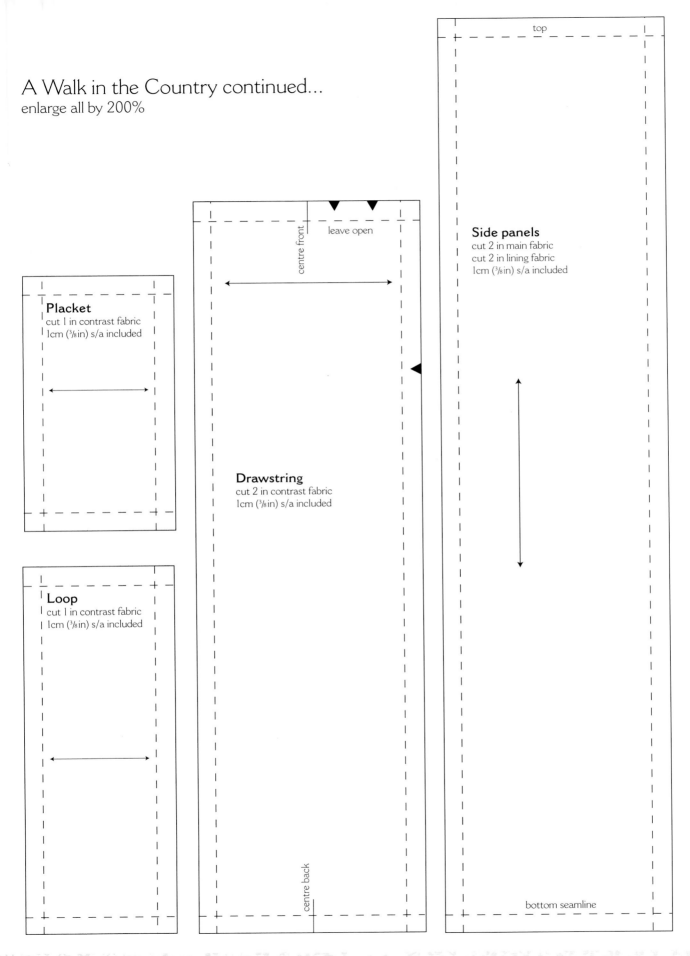

Placket
cut 1 in contrast fabric
1cm (⅜in) s/a included

Loop
cut 1 in contrast fabric
1cm (⅜in) s/a included

centre front

leave open

Drawstring
cut 2 in contrast fabric
1cm (⅜in) s/a included

centre back

top

Side panels
cut 2 in main fabric
cut 2 in lining fabric
1cm (⅜in) s/a included

bottom seamline

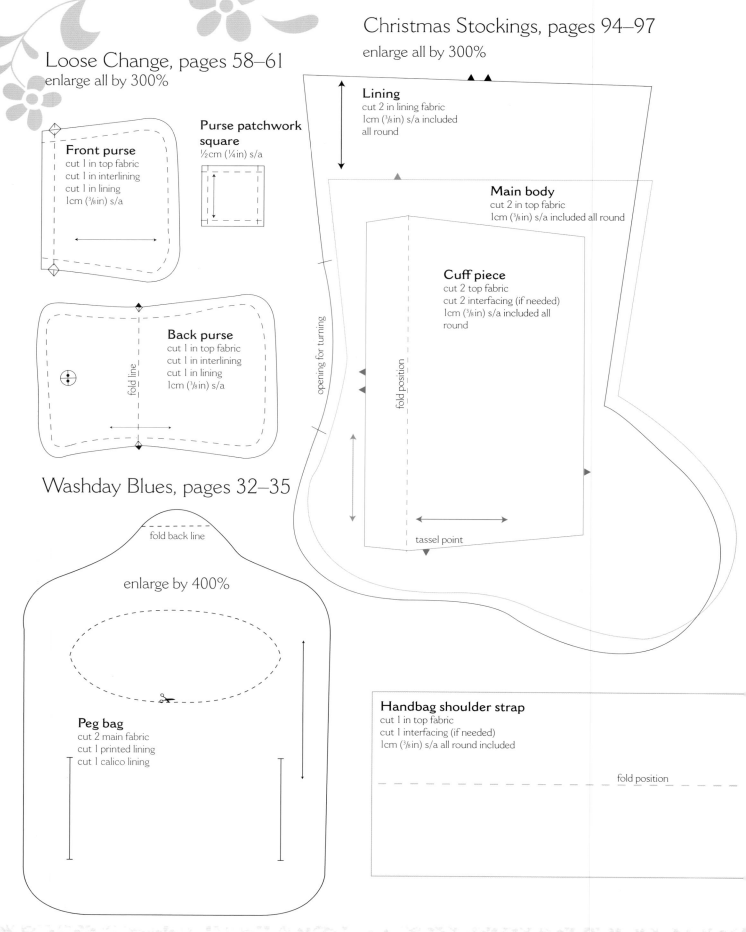

Loose Change, pages 58–61
enlarge all by 300%

Front purse
cut 1 in top fabric
cut 1 in interlining
cut 1 in lining
1cm (³⁄₈in) s/a

Purse patchwork square
½cm (¼in) s/a

Back purse
cut 1 in top fabric
cut 1 in interlining
cut 1 in lining
1cm (³⁄₈in) s/a

fold line

Washday Blues, pages 32–35

fold back line

enlarge by 400%

Peg bag
cut 2 main fabric
cut 1 printed lining
cut 1 calico lining

Christmas Stockings, pages 94–97
enlarge all by 300%

Lining
cut 2 in lining fabric
1cm (³⁄₈in) s/a included
all round

Main body
cut 2 in top fabric
1cm (³⁄₈in) s/a included all round

Cuff piece
cut 2 top fabric
cut 2 interfacing (if needed)
1cm (³⁄₈in) s/a included all
round

opening for turning

fold position

tassel point

Handbag shoulder strap
cut 1 in top fabric
cut 1 interfacing (if needed)
1cm (³⁄₈in) s/a all round included

fold position

Beautiful Bags 62–65
enlarge all by 200%

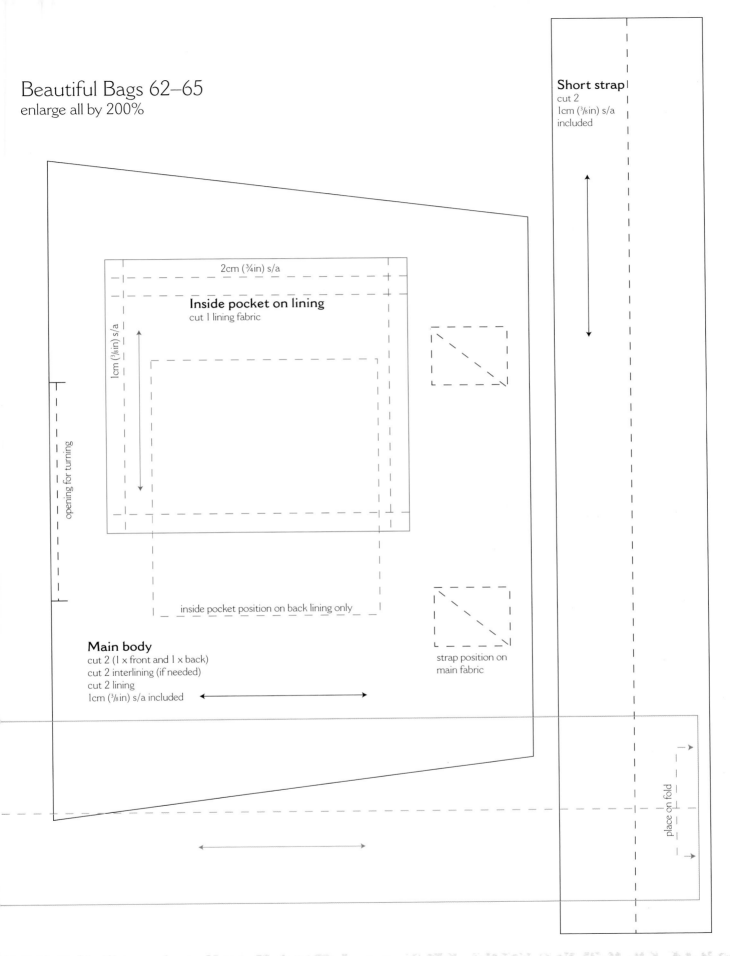

Short strap
cut 2
1cm (³⁄₈in) s/a
included

2cm (¾in) s/a

Inside pocket on lining
cut 1 lining fabric

1cm (³⁄₈in) s/a

opening for turning

inside pocket position on back lining only

Main body
cut 2 (1 x front and 1 x back)
cut 2 interlining (if needed)
cut 2 lining
1cm (³⁄₈in) s/a included

strap position on
main fabric

place on fold

Silas the Dog, pages 102–105
enlarge all by 300%

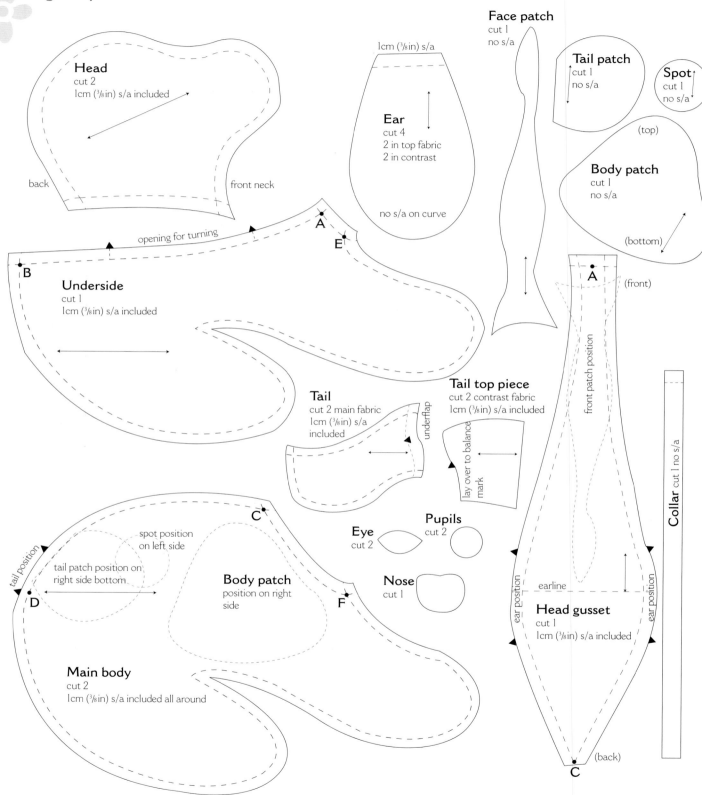

Head
cut 2
1cm (³⁄₈in) s/a included

back

front neck

opening for turning

Underside
cut 1
1cm (³⁄₈in) s/a included

B

A

E

Ear
cut 4
2 in top fabric
2 in contrast

no s/a on curve

1cm (³⁄₈in) s/a

Face patch
cut 1
no s/a

Tail patch
cut 1
no s/a

Spot
cut 1
no s/a

Body patch
cut 1
no s/a

(top)

(bottom)

(front)

A

front patch position

Tail
cut 2 main fabric
1cm (³⁄₈in) s/a included

Tail top piece
cut 2 contrast fabric
1cm (³⁄₈in) s/a included

underflap

lay over to balance mark

Collar cut 1 no s/a

tail position

spot position on left side

tail patch position on right side bottom

D

C

Body patch
position on right side

F

Eye
cut 2

Pupils
cut 2

Nose
cut 1

Main body
cut 2
1cm (³⁄₈in) s/a included all around

ear position

earline

ear position

Head gusset
cut 1
1cm (³⁄₈in) s/a included

(back)

C

A Cushion Full of Memories, pages 110–115
enlarge by 400%

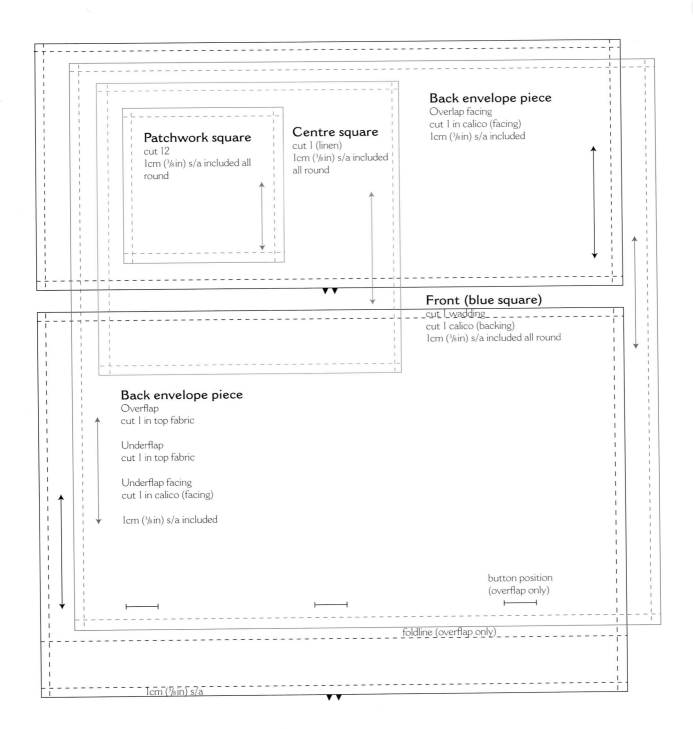

Patchwork square
cut 12
1cm (³/₈in) s/a included all round

Centre square
cut 1 (linen)
1cm (³/₈in) s/a included all round

Back envelope piece
Overlap facing
cut 1 in calico (facing)
1cm (³/₈in) s/a included

Front (blue square)
cut 1 wadding
cut 1 calico (backing)
1cm (³/₈in) s/a included all round

Back envelope piece
Overflap
cut 1 in top fabric

Underflap
cut 1 in top fabric

Underflap facing
cut 1 in calico (facing)

1cm (³/₈in) s/a included

button position
(overflap only)

foldline (overflap only)

1cm (³/₈in) s/a

As Tall as a House,
pages 106–109

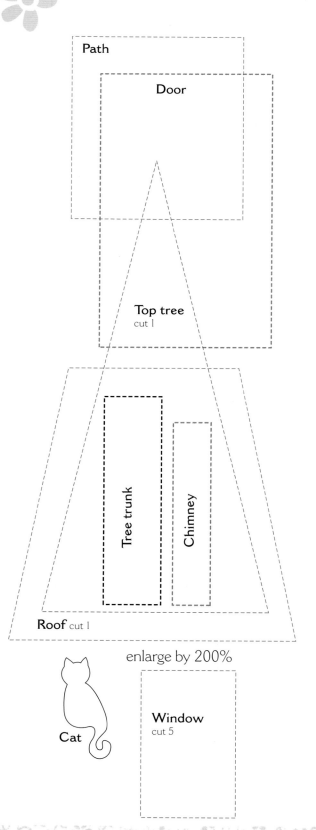

Path

Door

Top tree
cut 1

Tree trunk

Chimney

Roof cut 1

enlarge by 200%

Cat

Window
cut 5

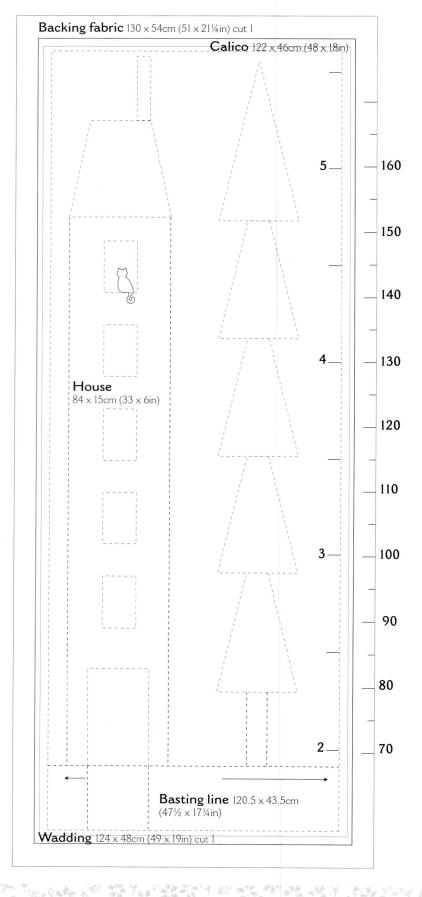

Backing fabric 130 × 54cm (51 × 21¼in) cut 1

Calico 122 × 46cm (48 × 18in)

House
84 × 15cm (33 × 6in)

Basting line 120.5 × 43.5cm
(47½ × 17¼in)

Wadding 124 × 48cm (49 × 19in) cut 1

5 — — 160

— 150

— 140

4 — — 130

— 120

— 110

— 100

— 90

3 — — 100

— 80

2 — — 70

Motif Templates
enlarge all by 300%

Cut 2
5mm (¼in) s/a

opening for turning through

Centre heart
cut 1 Bondaweb

Top

Cut 2
5mm (¼in) s/a

opening for turning through

Centre star
cut 1
Bondaweb

Cut 2
5mm (¼in) s/a

opening for turning through

Wing
cut 2
Bondaweb

About the Authors

Ginny Farquhar

Coming from a family who always made things, Ginny's love of fabrics started as a child. After training in theatrical costume at Wimbledon School of Art in London, UK, she enjoyed a successful career designing, making and teaching costume before settling in Hampshire, where she now lives with her husband Rod and daughters, Isabella and Imogen. A keen recycler and passionate grower of vegetables, Ginny loves to create and share ideas.

Alice Butcher

Alice trained as a printed textile designer before going on to run the prestigious Liberty of London Sewing School and later setting up a complementary quarterly sewing magazine. She has always had a great passion for colour and fabrics and is never happier than when she is working at the studio she shares with Ginny, creating new and exciting things. She lives in Farnham, Surrey with her husband Nick, their two children, Oscar and Ned and of course, Silas the dog.

Alice and Ginny have run a successful crafting business, folkydokee, for a number of years and exhibited at the Hampton Court Flower Show, Country Living Fairs and House and Garden fairs in the UK. They now work together as "Alice and Ginny" and are undertaking many new and exciting projects. For more information see www.aliceandginny.co.uk.

Suppliers

US Suppliers

Beadbox
1290 N. Scottsdale Road
Tempe Arizona 85281-1703
Tel: 1-800-232-3269
www.beadbox.com

Distinctive Fabric
2023 Bay Street
Los Angeles
CA 90021
Tel: 877 721 7269
www.distinctivefabric.com

Gütermann of America Inc
8227 Arrowbridge Blvd
PO Box 7387
Charlotte
NC 28241-7387
Tel: (704) 525 7068
Email: info@gutermann-us.com

J&O Fabrics
9401 Rt.130
Pennsauken
NJ 08110
Tel: 856 663 2121
Website: www.jandofabrics.com

Purl Patchwork
147 Sullivan Street
New York, NY 10012
Tel: (212) 420-879
www.purlsoho.com
Retail fabrics

Reprodepot Fabrics
Website: www.reprodepot.com
Online retail of vintage reproduction and retro fabrics and embellishments

Tinsel Trading Company
47 West 38th Street
New York, NY 10018
www.tinseltrading.com
Retail flowers, trims and tassels

UK Suppliers

Beadworks
16 Redbridge Enterprise Centre
Thompson Close, Ilford
Essex, IG1 1TY
www.beadworks.co.uk *Retail and wholesale beads, brooch backs and twine*

Carnmeal Cottage
Carnmeal Downs
Breage, Helston
Cornwall, TR13 9NL
www.carnmeal.com
Retail and wholesale craft supplies

Fabricland
Fabric Towers, Kingfisher Park
Headland, Salisbury Road
Ringwood, BH24 3NX
www.fabricland.co.uk
Retail dress and craft fabrics, haberdashery and trimmings

Groves and Bank
Drakes Drive Industrial Estate
Long Crendon, Aylesbury
HP18 9BA
www.groves-banks.com
Wholesale haberdashery

Habico
Tong Road Industrial Estate
Amberley Road
Leeds, LS12 4BD
www.habico.co.uk
Wholesale haberdashery, trimmings, card blanks, Bondaweb

John Kaldor
Portland House
4 Great Portland Street
London, W1W 8QJ
www.johnkaldor.co.uk
Wholesale dress fabrics

John Lewis
Draycott Avenue,
London, SW3 2NA
www.johnlewis.com
Retail craft, dress and furnishing fabric and haberdashery

Kleins
5 Noel Street
London, W1F 8GD
www.kleins.co.uk
Wholesale trimmings

Loop Fabrics
32 West Hill Road
Brighton, BN1 3RT
www.loopfabric.co.uk
Retail and wholesale organic and sustainable fabrics including cotton and hemp

Morplan Ltd
PO Box 54
Harlow
Essex
CM20 2TS
www.morplan.com
Retail and wholesale suppliers, wooden coat hangers, pattern-cutting equipment

Whaleys
Harris Court, Great Horton
Bradford, BD7 4EQ
www.whaleys-bradford.ltd.uk
Wholesale and retail fabric, canvas, interlinings and interfacing

Also check out charity shops and thrift stores for good-quality clothing, table linens, soft furnishings, remnants and buttons.

Acknowledgments

We would like to say a big thank you to our families and friends for sharing our enthusiasm for this book and for making us keep at it! We would also like to thank everyone at David and Charles, particularly Ali, for giving us this wonderful opportunity and believing in us. Thanks also to Isabella, Oscar, Imogen, Ned, Hayden and Tess for being such great models and to Simon for his wonderful photography.

Index